Robert H.I. Palgrave

The Local Taxation of Great Britain and Ireland

Robert H.I. Palgrave

The Local Taxation of Great Britain and Ireland

ISBN/EAN: 9783337322748

Printed in Europe, USA, Canada, Australia, Japan

Cover: Foto ©Suzi / pixelio.de

More available books at **www.hansebooks.com**

THE

·LOCAL TAXATION

OF

GREAT BRITAIN AND IRELAND:

By ROBERT HARRY INGLIS PALGRAVE,

Member of the Council of the Statistical Society of London.

The very best of all plans of finance is to spend little, and the best taxation of all is that which is
least in amount.—SAY.

LONDON:

JOHN MURRAY, ALBEMARLE STREET.

1871.

PREFACE.

—◆—

THE Local Administration of this country has been much discussed in recent years, and when Mr. Tayler offered the prize which was the immediate occasion of the following pages, I gladly undertook to investigate a complete field of inquiry, many parts of which had interested me before. While writing, I was entirely unacquainted with the exhaustive report on the subject, then being drawn up under the direction of the Right Hon. G. J. Goschen. My Essay was submitted to the Council of the Statistical Society on 31st January, 1871, and the award of the adjudicators was made on 20th March, while Mr. Goschen's report did not appear till 3rd April. Although thus I had not the advantage which the possession of Mr. Goschen's report would have been to me at the time, there appeared to be no reason why such additional information as space permitted, should not be obtained from that report and incorporated here. The quotations made from that report have all been carefully marked, and the fullest information on the subject, obtainable at the present time, is thus given. It is needful to add the words "at the "present time," for as yet complete details do not exist of all branches of Local Taxation throughout the United Kingdom.

As a disposition has been manifested to endeavour to alter the basis on which some rates are levied, it is desirable to draw attention to the fact that the apparent inequality of Local Taxation lies, not so much in the method of raising the sums imposed, as in the manner in which those sums are expended. Local rates in England are all levied on the

occupier, but they are, in Towns especially, expended in
great degree upon objects which ultimately benefit not the
occupier but the owner; while in the Rural districts, the
owner is at least as much interested as the occupier in keeping down charges which affect the permanent value of his
property.

Again, of those charges which fairly belong to the occupier as such, many are for imperial, not merely local, matters.
Local rates have been too much considered in this country
as forming a convenient fund on which any charge might be
imposed, which it was not desirable to defray from the
imperial taxes. That the expenditure for the relief of the
poor is best directed by local knowledge and experience is
beyond doubt, but these qualities can be but of small service
in administering many other charges which are at present
paid out of the rates. To settle an equitable division
between local and imperial expenses is therefore eminently
desirable, and should precede a division of the rates between
owner and occupier. Together with these points the incidence of imperial taxation on the different classes of ratepayers must be thoroughly examined into, that fairness in
the apportionment of this taxation may be obtained.

It appeared to me that in carrying out this inquiry it was
best to give, besides a short historical statement of the mode
in which the existing system had grown up, a statistical
account of the various rates levied. This method alone supplies the required information about a system of taxation
which, though based on one uniform plan, falls with an
apparent inequality of incidence on different places in the
same country. Hence a vast amount of detail was needed,
and a considerable number of tables had to be prepared. Of
these tables the most important have been selected, and are
published here. They may be considered as forming a chart

indicating the pressure of local taxation throughout England, and not only afford the means of comparing the incidence of the main branches of local taxation between one place and another, but of observing what the effect would be if the local rates were levied on all descriptions of property instead of those at present included in the assessment.

The effect of levying local taxation on the income and property tax assessments for each county, is shown in several tables; the results to average individuals would probably be nearly identical with those at present prevailing, but with all the disadvantages which a high rate of income tax always brings. The burdensome character of the taxation of personal property in America may be also referred to here, as affording an example to be avoided.

The numerous subjects branching out of the main question—subjects which it was impossible either to disregard entirely, or to discuss fully—account for the form in which the present work appears.

A complete table of contents as well as an alphabetical index is given. Besides a general statement of the principal local taxes, the objects for which they are raised, and the authorities by which they are levied and expended, the most prominent instances of the disadvantages of the present system of local administration are referred to. Those cases also in which the existing method of rating involves an apparent inequality, for instance, in the assessment of railways, canals, and gas companies, and, in some cases, of tithes, are mentioned.

I feel that in endeavouring to investigate these great and difficult questions, I have hardly done so in a manner equal to the importance of the subject, but at least I have desired to fulfil my work in a complete way, and in a spirit of fairness. Throughout, the points involved have been

treated from a Statistical, and not from a Political, point
of view. It will be a satisfaction to me if my work contribute, in any degree, to the solution of difficulties now
acknowledged to be pressing, and some of national importance. It will be a further satisfaction if, concurrently with
this, it should assist at all the progress of statistical inquiry,
a method which, though scarcely receiving at the present
time the attention it deserves, has this advantage, that,
fairly followed out, it enables the inquirer into those subjects
which admit of investigation by simple enumeration, to
arrive by patient study, at the facts of each case.

R. H. I. P.

October, 1871.

THE

LOCAL TAXATION

OF

GREAT BRITAIN AND IRELAND.

CONTENTS:

An ALPHABETICAL INDEX *of the principal subjects will be found at* p. 121.

" The very best of all plans of finance is to spend little, and the best **taxation**
" of all is that which is least in amount."—Say.

I.—INTRODUCTION.

Judged by this golden maxim the local taxation of England can
hardly be called successful. It is certain that far from little is
spent, and it is equally certain that a very large proportion of the
taxes levied, is required for local purposes. The local administration
of England is peculiarly open to both these objections. Scotland
and Ireland both appear to be more fortunate in their systems of
local government, and in the consequent economy to taxpayers in
those parts of the United Kingdom. It is not only recently that
the complaint of the heavy demands made by the local tax gatherer
has arisen in this country. More than forty years ago the poor's
rates in England and Wales reached so high an amount that a
revision of the system under which they were administered was
imperatively called for. The Poor Law Amendment Act was passed
in 1834, and for the time a great economy ensued.

The poor's rates in England fell, in the space from between 1834
and 1837, from 6,317,255*l.* (1834) to 4,044,741*l.* (1837). The
number of paupers was reduced, and the general prosperity of the
country greatly augmented.

The complaint is now not so much as in 1834, of the poor's rate,
though the poor's rate has, during the last few years, unfortunately
increased not only in amount, but in proportion both to the value of
property assessed, and to the population,* as of all local taxes col-
lectively. These taxes are at the present so high that they amount
to more than a third of the taxation imposed for the general purposes
of the government—those imposts which, for the sake of clearness,
may be best termed imperial taxes—while the expenditure, including
the amounts raised by loans, is nearly the half of that of the central
authorities.†

* *Vide* " Poor Law Board Report, 1869-70," p. xvii :—

Year.	Rate per Head of Amount Expended in Poor Relief on the Estimated Population.	Year.	Rate in the £ of Poor Relief.
	s. d.		*s. d.*
1866	6 1¼	1866	1 4·5
'69	7 -¾	'68	1 5·9

† As an illustration of the amount of similar taxation in other places, a comparison between the taxes in New York State and Great Britain (1867) is given,
Appendix III.

B

Mr. Goschen's estimate is as follows :—

" Though my special intention has been to inquire into the local
" taxation of England and Wales, I have collected as much infor-
" mation as was accessible to me as regards Scotland and Ireland.
" Statements IX and X, in Part I of Appendix A, show the aggregate
" amount of local receipts and expenditure for Scotland and Ireland
" respectively.   They are as follows :—

	£
Local expenditure in Scotland (partly estimated)	3,000,000
„ Ireland	3,050,000
If to these amounts we add the English expenditure of	30,240,000
We arrive at the total of	36,290,000

" as the aggregate local expenditure of the United Kingdom."—
" Report on Local Taxation, 1870," p. 6.

It is scarcely possible to consider the local taxation of the
country altogether apart from the taxes raised by the imperial
government ; but, as it is the local taxation principally to which
attention is now directed, reference to the imperial taxation of the
country is only made when needed for purposes of illustration, or
when the two branches of the subject are so closely interwoven that
they have to be examined together.

The returns recently made by order of the House of Commons
contain the fullest and most reliable information yet obtained on
local taxation.   The difficulties attending a complete investigation
of the subject are well illustrated by these returns, which fully
support, even in their present comparatively complete state, the
remarks in the accompanying quotation from M. de Parieu's admi-
rable treatise on taxation :—

" Si en effet tout ce qui concerne les revenues nationaux tend
" aujourd'hui, dans toute l'Europe, à se divulger et à se produire
" dans des budgets communiqués au public, la taxation locale se
" cache au contraire dans l'ombre et il suffira, pour expliquer la
" difficulté d'atteindre les faits qui s'y rattachent, de faire remarquer
" quelle place restreinte tiennent dans nos documens officiels les
" ressources, cependant si considérables et si variées, fournies en
" France par l'octroi, les centimes additionnels, les droits de voiries
" et de places, etc., aux caises municipales."

" A cause de cette subordination des taxes locales aux taxes
" générales, les premières semblent avoir souvent un caractère
" d'imperfection speciale, qui résulte d'une culture d'esprit un peu
" moins parfaite chez ceux qui les votent, et souvent de leur
" ancienneté, qui les destine à représenter, pour ainsi dire, l'archaïsme
" de la taxation."—From "Traité des Impots," par M. Esquiron de
Parieu, vol. iv, pp. 4 and 5.

The returns cited extend only to England and Wales, nor, when first issued, did they give exact information even for those portions of the United Kingdom. A memorandum in Return No. 497—I contains amendments in part of No. 497; No. 430 contains a further amendment still, nor can the latest of these papers, though carefully drawn up, be said to give all the information that might be desired with respect to local revenues. Those imposts which are raised by municipalities otherwise than by way of rates do not appear in these returns.

Fair, market, bridge and ferry, harbour, and light dues are excluded, probably as being considered charges for services rendered. In those cases, however, in which a surplus revenue remains after defraying the charges incurred, these dues are distinctly taxes. Their omission is to be regretted, as thus the statement of local revenue and local expenditure is therefore to this extent incomplete.* The amounts raised in London in this manner are so large, that it is desirable to give some particulars of them.

* A memorandum in Return No. 497—I, p. v, gives these items as below for the year 1867 :—

	£
Markets and fairs	26,282
Bridges and ferries	110,835
Harbours	1,259,990
Turnpike tolls	970,925
Pilotage and light dues	612,437
	2,980,469

In Mr. Goschen's return, the sum under these heads, "principally for the year 1868, or for the year ending 31st March, 1869 " (pp. 58—60), are :—

	£
Markets and fairs	64,198
Bridges and ferries	134,572
Harbours	1,945,805
Turnpike trusts	1,023,563
Pilotage authorities	332,083
Light dues, &c.	379,525
	3,879,746

The amounts in Mr. Goschen's return include " sums borrowed," principally on account of harbour and turnpike authorities. The discrepancy between these two sets of figures is thus mainly, though by no means entirely, accounted for. Both returns are published by authority of the Government ; the difference between them serves to illustrate the difficulties experienced by the inquirer into these subjects.

As these amounts are not distributed to their respective localities in the three Returns of Local Taxation (Nos. 497, 497—I, and 430), which have been mainly employed as the basis of this work, and it may be questioned how far the sums are paid by the inhabitants of the places where collected, these dues are only referred to in the general summary, p. 2

Summary of the Accounts of the Corporation of London for 1868 and 1869.

	Receipts.		Expenditure.	
	1868.	1869.	1868.	1869.
	£	£	£	£
The City's estate account	399,857	279,858	380,590	322,706
Reserve fund	—	17,406	—	128,008
Billingsgate Market tolls	—	193	677	766
City's 4d. coal duty	79,466	91,734	103,790	119,045
Bridge House estates.......	242,449	45,427	245,712	53,838
Rebuilding Blackfriars Bridge....	100	50,107	54,442	56,934
Metropolitan Meat and Poultry } Market (site and approaches } and tolls account) .... }	—	248,850	26,184	117,529
Ditto (western approach)............	129	201,122	22,562	143,588
Newgate Market fund	—	—	—	92
Holborn Valley improvement	563,053	706,144	375,867	705,158
Commissioners of Sewers, No. 1	220,737	156,935	258,437	157,787
„ 2	35,180	28,907	26,622	34,901
„ 3	35,552	32,036	54,139	28,572
Police fund...............................	56,607	50,183	64,786	66,247
Ward rates	4,904	4,906	3,979	5,088
Police superannuation	3,583	3,175	4,248	4,472
Wine duty and 9d. coal duty	195,854	197,707	192,049	194,559
Drawback on coals.......................	2,780	2,718	2,612	2,221
Coal duties expenses fund...........	—	—	5,642	5,268
„ Market fund	2,351	2,295	2,619	2,357
Farringdon Street improvements	5,246	5,876	3,384	3,028
West end of Cheapside im- } provement .... }	427	1,009	13	23
General fund of City of Lon- } don Court .... }	7,948	9,413	7,539	8,952
Accumulated surplus profits } of Chamberlain's Office........ }	2,065	4,569	2,000	4,634
Profits of „	21,519	16,061	6,156	5,853
Town clerk's establishment	18	18	—	—
Total	1,879,825	2,156,649	1,844,049	2,171,626

In Liverpool also, to name only one of the most prominent instances, large sums are raised for the benefit of the municipality, which do not enter into these returns. Nor can any statement be considered complete which does not include those revenues which many municipal bodies receive from property belonging to their respective boroughs.

In a complete investigation, these other points ought to be included. Information about them is for every reason very desirable.*

* As an example, the borough of Beccles, in the county of Suffolk, with a population of 4,841 (Census 1871), possessed, in 1870, a net income arising from property of more than 2,000l. per annum, from which the expenses of the roads and streets, the public lighting, police, and other similar charges, were defrayed, and a considerable surplus devoted to the public improvements of the borough. This instance is given as one of a class; in illustration also of the general principle that where public interests, in places of small extent, are concerned, public revenues are generally best administered by those personally interested in keeping down local charges.

A return also of the loans raised by the different local boards and authorities is also greatly needed, together with a statement of the arrangements for a sinking fund (where such exists), and of the proportion of the debt still unredeemed at the date of making the return.

The report of the evidence given before a select committee appointed by the House of Commons, 21st February, 1870, "To " inquire and report whether it is expedient that the charges now " locally imposed on the occupiers of rateable property should be " divided between the owners and occupiers, and what changes in " the constitution of the local bodies, now administering rates, " should follow such division," affords the most recent information obtainable, besides that contained in the returns named. This committee, presided over by Mr. Goschen as chairman, in the course of their inquiry examined many witnesses unusually well qualified to give evidence on the subject. Thus, Mr. Danby P. Fry, of the legal department of the Poor Law Board; Mr. Tom Taylor, secretary of the Local Government Act office; the late Sir John Thwaites, then chairman of the Metropolitan Board of Works; Dr. W. Neilson Hancock, the head of the Statistical Department in Ireland; Mr. James Caird, C.B.; Mr. C. S. Read, M.P.; Mr. R. Dudley Baxter; Sir Sydney H. Waterlow; Mr. C. G. Gray; Mr. H. Arthur Hunt; Mr. H. Christie Beloe; and several others, were all examined. Evidence was given as to the effect of rates in town and country, in the metropolis, in large cities like Liverpool, in counties as differently circumstanced as Lancashire and Wiltshire. The report to which the committee agreed, illustrated so clearly the difficulties that exist in dealing with the subject, that it is given below in full.* Before considering it in detail, it will be desirable to refer to some of the main points involved. First among these stands the manner in which the required amounts are raised. The taxation for this purpose is, with exceptions so few that they may be disregarded in taking a broad view of the question, entirely direct. It is raised by rates, on one kind of property alone, though not on all that kind of property. This arrangement may be said to be universally employed in raising local taxation in Great Britain.

The functions of the local administrator are thus limited, so far as raising a revenue is concerned, to one point, the making sure that the sum required will be obtained. The State, while entrusting to the local authorities the duty of raising a sufficient revenue, restricts the method in which the tax shall be levied to one particular head of property. All the advantages enjoyed by the Chancellor of the Exchequer of the State in the power of levying indirect taxation, are thus denied to the authority whom one may term the chancellor of the exchequer of the borough or county. The Chancellor of the

* *Vide* Appendix, No. VIII.

Exchequer of the State endeavours to adjust the taxes which he imposes, so as to meet the various capabilities of the subjects of the realm to bear individually their share of the burden. In the words of Mr. Gladstone in his budget speech, 18th April, 1853, "While " we have sought to do justice to the great labouring community of " England by further extending their relief from indirect taxation, " we have not been guided by any desire to set one class against " another; we have felt we should best maintain our own honour, " that we should best meet the views of Parliament, and best pro- " mote the interests of the country, by declining to draw any " invidious distinction between class and class, by adopting it to " ourselves as a sacred aim, to diffuse and distribute, burden if we " must, benefit if we may, with equal and impartial hand ; and we " have the consolation of believing that by proposals such as these " we contribute as far as in us lies, not only to develope the material " resources of the country, but to knit the hearts of the various " classes of this great nation yet more closely than heretofore to " that throne and to those institutions under which it is their hap- " piness to live." These advantages are denied to the local admi- nistrator. Equally so is the power of inducing an increase of revenue by a remission of taxation. How many times within our memory, and within the limits of modern financial legislation, has an in- creased revenue been obtained after a diminution in the percentage of the levy, the stimulus given to the permanent prosperity of the State more than compensating the temporary loss to the exchequer. This advantage is not possessed by the local authority. No diminu- tion in rating which he can suggest will suffice to enhance the prosperity of the taxpayer to such an extent as to produce any recuperative return. The only assistance which the local revenue can receive is from the natural increase in the local resources arising from the augmentation in the numbers and prosperity of the population. The increase in value of rateable property in this country has been very considerable.

" The following table exhibits the progress in value of real " property from 1815 downwards, correcting the figure for 1815 as " regards rateable value in the manner indicated :—

	Annual Value.	Rateable Value.	Proportion of Rateable Value to Income Tax Assessment.
	£	£	Per cnt.
1815...............	53,495,000 {	40,121,000 (estimated)	75 (estimated)
'41–43	85,802,000	62,540,000	72·89
'47.................	89,759,000	67,320,000	75·03
'56..	102,221,000	71,840,000	70·25
'68..................	143,872,000	100,612,000	70·00

" An examination of these figures will show the following
" result:—

" The annual value of property assessed under Schedule (A),
" has increased about 169 per cent. between 1815 and 1868; and in
" the rateable value there has been an increase of about 150 per
" cent. Since the year 1841 there has been an increase in the
" annual value of about 68 per cent., and in the rateable value of
" about 61 per cent. But, as the rates in the pound have for the
" year 1815 been calculated, not on the 40,121,000*l.*, which analogy
" would show to have been the rateable value in 1813-15, but on
" 51,898,000*l.*, I shall have to deal mainly with the latter figure.
" If this figure truly represented the rateable value in 1815, the
" increase in rateable value would not have been 150 per cent., but
" 94 per cent. If the former figure is correct, 23 per cent. would
" have to be added to be recorded rates in the pound quoted in the
" old returns for 1813-15.

" The same figure, 51,898,000*l.*, has been taken in the old re-
" turns for the year 1826-27, by which time the value of property
" must have much increased.

" We know that the rateable value in 1841 was 62,540,000*l.* As
" the year 1826-27 lies about halfway between 1814 and 1841, the
" figure of 51,898,000*l.* appears to be a fairly correct amount for
" the year 1826-27, being a middle term between our estimate of
" 40,121,000*l.* for 1813-15, and the ascertained figure of 62,540,000*l.*
" for 1841.

" The general result is sufficiently distinct; the rateable value of
" real property has been increased from 40,000,000*l.* to 100,000,000*l.*,
" an increase of 150 per cent. (If the sum of 50,000,000*l.* be taken
" as the rateable value for 1815, the increase has been 100 per
" cent.) The annual value has been increased by a sum of about
" 90,000,000*l.* sterling, or nearly 170 per cent.

" Since 1841 the increase has been 38,000,000*l.* in rateable
" value, and 58,000,000*l.* in annual value, showing respectively an
" increase of 61 and 68 per cent."—" Report on Local Taxation,
" No. 470, 1870."—*Mr. Goschen.*

Table M, compiled from other sources, and drawn up independently from Mr. Goschen's, confirms this estimate.

Other points for consideration also occur; for instance, the
reasons which call for an increase in the rates reflect themselves
likewise adversely in the condition of the ratepayer. Work is
scarce, and the poor rates increase. The ratepayer has felt the evil
as rapidly as the pauper, and is the less able to meet the enhanced
outlay. Sanitary measures require higher local taxation. The ratepayer has suffered alike with the non-ratepayer, in purse if not in
person. It should always be borne in mind that the same person
generally contributes to both funds, to those raised by local, and

imperial taxation, and in different ratios; that the local taxation, being direct, is an impost which the ratepayer can in no way avoid, as he may a portion of the imperial taxation, by abstaining from using the articles subject to it. There are some objections to this system of laying rates only on "visible" and "real" estate. Some of these disadvantages will be examined into further on. But it is probable that the existing system will be maintained. The taxes raised are so large that their very amount almost of itself precludes any reconstitution of the existing plan which would propose to raise these sums, or any large proportion of them, by any other method.

· " The argument for a tax, or mode of taxation, that it exists, is " always a very strong one, when the abolition would necessitate other " taxes to supply its place. The mere antiquity of the system by " giving time for the adjustment of the burden on the subject taxed " makes it fall lighter, very much lighter, than any novel tax or " method possibly could, and rates on real property, continuing " from generation to generation without material increase, are not " less but more likely than most taxes to show the effect of this " adjustment." The fact that local taxes have recently greatly increased, and that it is probable that they will shortly experience a considerable further increase,* renders an inquiry into the subject at the present time highly expedient.

" Materials, more or less perfect, exist for instituting com- " parisons between the extent of local burdens at the following " dates:—1803, the average of 1813-15, 1817, 1826-27, 1841, 1862, " and 1868. But the fact that the same rates were at some dates " collected with the poor rate, and returned with them, and at other " times levied separately, causes considerable confusion, and some " uncertainty.

" The receipts from rates, as far as they can be ascertained, " amounted (for England and Wales)—

	£		£
In 1803 to	5,348,000	In 1841 to	8,101,000
„ '13–15 to	8,164,000	„ '51 „	8,916,000
„ '17 to	10,107,000	„ '62 „	12,207,000
„ '26–27 to	9,544,000	„ '68 „	16,800,000
		(inclusive of church rates.)	

" 1. The aggregate local expenditure of the United Kingdom is " upwards of 36,000,000l.

" 2. The aggregate local expenditure of England and Wales, in

* An estimate, framed by Sir S. H. Northcote (Table R), gives the local tax- ation of Great Britain and Ireland for 1860, as about 15,700,000l. An estimate in the "Statistical Abstract," No. 17, states the corresponding amount in 1870, as 25,000,000l. According to Mr. Goschen's report, the actual expenditure in 1868-69 was 36,290,000l., the amounts raised by *rates* being 16,200,000l. in England and Wales, 1,500,000l. in Scotland, and 2,280,000l. in Ireland.

" a given year (1868), was 30,240,000*l.*; the receipts for the same
" year being 30,140,000*l.**

" 3. Of this sum—

£
16,200,000 or	53·5 per cent.	are raised by rates, being direct local taxation
4,350,000 ,,	14·2 ,,	,, tolls, dues, fees, being indirect local taxation
1,325,000 ,,	4·2 ,,	,, sales or rents of property
1,225,000 ,,	4·0 ,,	,, Government subvention
5,500,000 ,,	19·0 ,,	varied by loans
1,540,000 ,,	5·1 ,,	raised by miscellaneous receipts

30,140,000   100·0

" 4. Of the aggregate receipts of 30,140,000*l.*—

£
13,000,000 or	43·1 per cent.	are spent in distinctly *urban* districts
5,030,000 ,,	16·8 ,,	,, *rural* districts
9,470,000 ,,	31·3 ,,	in districts *partly rural partly urban*
2,640,000 ,,	8·8 ,,	by *maritime authorities*

30,140,000   100·0

" I now leave the subject of the total actual revenue and expen-
" diture of local authorities in order to deal more especially with
" 'the rates.'

" Taking the same distribution of rates, as has been made of
" the total local receipts between the various classes of authorities,
" we have the following result:—

	Rates.	
Purely Urban Authorities—	£	£
Municipal boroughs	914,000	
Improvement Commissioners	410,000	
Local boards	1,685,000	
Vestries, &c. (metropolis)	1,036,000	
City of London	175,000	
Metropolitan Board of Works........................	417,000	
Metropolitan police	482,000	
Total	5,119,000	5,119,000
Purely Rural Authorities—		
County treasurers	1,501,000	
Highway authorities......................................	1,378,000	
Lighting and watching..................................	80,000	
Commissioners of Sewers (extra-metropolitan)	43,000	
Drainage and embankment (extra-metropolitan)	176,000	
Total	3,178,000	3,178,000
Partly Urban partly Rural Authorities—		
Boards of guardians......................................	7,830,000	
Burial boards	96,000	
Total	7,926,000	7,926,000
Total of rates levied by all authorities....	—	16,223,000

—" Report on Local Taxation, 1870."

* The difference must have been provided for by balances.

It must be borne in mind that an over oppressive taxation may become so onerous, as to be not merely without benefit to the revenue but conducive to its loss.*

As there appears to be an impression in some quarters that local taxation has on some occasions reached so high a point, that land has occasionally been allowed to go out of cultivation in consequence of the inadequacy of the produce to meet the charges levied thereon, it is as well to mention that no distinct proof appears to exist that such has been the case. In the evidence taken by the agricultural committees in 1836, the leading questions were clearly intended to elicit answers which should tend to prove that cultivation was undergoing diminution or deterioration, but it was only in isolated cases, and under peculiar circumstances, that cultivation could be shown to have either been deteriorated or diminished. Those peculiar circumstances seem to have applied chiefly to some parts of Buckinghamshire and Yorkshire. With reference to the latter, one of the witnesses, Mr. C. Howard, states that some of the poor strong soils of Howdenshire had gone out of cultivation, not, however, in consequence of the low prices of 1832 to 1836, but in consequence of the wet seasons (notwithstanding the high prices) of 1829-30-31.†

" A point has been reached in many localities beyond which it " is hardly possible the rates can be raised, and it would not be " judicious to raise them, yet the necessities of local taxation are " increasing, more money is going out by the present channels, and " a totally new branch of expenditure, viz., for education, is imme- " diately in prospect."—"Economist," 16th May, 1868. At the same time it is probable, for the reasons just stated, that there will still remain a substantial body of rates on real property to form the subject of better arrangement.

Having thus briefly stated the manner in which local taxation generally is raised, and the increase which it has recently experienced, it is desirable to enter on the consideration of two of the main points of the subject. These are: the rates which are levied, and the constitution of the authorities by which they are levied. As the local taxation is levied mainly on one branch of property, namely, on real estate, it might have been expected that the method of raising the sums required would have been equally simple. But instead there are almost as many taxes in the local as in the imperial code.

---

* See remarks, in Appendix VII, on Taxation in Holland.

† "Tooke's History of Prices," vol. iii, pp. 42 and 43. Agricultural Report of the Committee of the House of Commons, 1836, questions 5346 to 5348.

II.—*General Outline of Principal Local Taxes.*

The principal rates levied for local purposes are:--

CLASS I.

Rates levied in primary districts, such as a parish.

1. *The Poor Rate.*
2. *The Highway Rate.*
3. *The Burial Board Rate.*
4. *The Lighting and Watching Rate.*
5. *The General District Rate.*
6. *The Sewerage Rate.*
7. *The Towns Improvement Rate.*
8. *The Animals Contagious Diseases Rate.*
9. *The Church Rate.*
10. *The Sewers Rate.*
11. *The General Sewers Rate.*
12. *The Drainage Embankment and Enclosure Rate.*

Rates levied in aggregate districts, such as a county.

1. The County Rates.
2. The Hundred Rate.
3. The Borough Rates.

This list, however, by no means exhausts the whole number; a complete list of all the several local rates is given in the Appendix to the Report of the Select Committee. The summary in Mr. Goschen's Report of 1870 gives a clear idea of the vast interests administered by these authorities.

" In order, therefore, to arrive at a clear conception of the whole " extent of local finance, it became necessary to institute an " exhaustive and minute inquiry into every source of local revenue. " The aggregate amounts received and expended in a given year by " each class of local authority in England and Wales, reaches the " astounding totals of 30,140,000*l.* of receipts, and 30,240,000*l.* of " expenditure. No comment is needed on the importance of the " considerations which this result of my inquiry suggests. The " bodies entrusted with the management of these funds form twenty " classes, as follows :—

	£
1. Board of guardians, responsible for the expenditure of receipts amounting to..	9,070,000
2. County magistrates and county treasurers, responsible for the expenditure of receipts amounting to	2,300,000

" Then follow seven classes of authorities exclu-
" sively *urban* in character :—

£

3. Municipal boroughs £2,710,000
4. Improvement commissioners 1,580,000
5. Local boards.. 2,500,000
6. Vestries, &c., of the metropolis................... 1,420,000
7. City of London Corporation and other ⎱ 1,830,000
    city trusts .... ⎰
8. Metropolitan Board of Works 2,110,000
9. The Metropolitan Police Commissioners 820,000
                       Total, about ———— 13,000,000

" The next two classes are—

10. Commissioners of Sewers (extra-⎱
    metropolitan) .... ⎰ receiving ⎱
11. Drainage and embankment autho- ⎰ together about ⎰ 230,000
    rities (extra-metropolitan)............⎰

" Then follow—

12. Lighting and watching authorities, under the old ⎱ 80,000
    Act of 3 and 4 Wm. IV, cap. 90, receiving............⎰
13. Burial boards, receiving 210,000

" Then follow two classes of authorities having
" under their charge the repair of roads, namely—

14. Highway authorities ⎱ receiving together 2,420,000
15. Turnpike trusts   ⎰

" Lastly, we have five other classes of bodies who
" administer mostly indirect taxes, namely—

16. Markets and fair authorities, receiving........................... 60,000
17. Bridges and ferries, receiving 130,000
18. Harbour authorities ....⎱
19. Pilotage   ,, ... ⎰ receiving together 2,640,000
20. Mercantile marine fund ⎰

            Total 30,140,000

" Looking broadly at these results, it may be well to bear in
" mind the following facts:—

£

Distinctly urban authorities receive 13,000,000
    ,,   rural   ,, ... 5,030,000

                              18,030,000

i.e. Road authorities.................................... £2,420,000
     County   ,, ... 2,300,000
     Lighting and watching authorities 80,000
     Drainage authorities 230,000

                         5,030,000

Authorities partly urban, partly rural, receive 9,470,000
  i.e. Boards of guardians £9,070,000
     Burial boards 210,000
     Bridges, ferries, market dues............... 190,000

                         9,470,000

Maritime authorities receive.. 2,640,000

           Total 30,140,000

" Nothing can be more important than that these broad lines of
" division should be borne clearly in mind. It may not be unneces-
" sary to repeat that the sums specified here as received by each
" class of local authority, include the proceeds of loans and other
" sources of revenue, as well as the sums raised by rates."*

These sums, whether derived from rates or loans, are raised for
purposes differing very widely from each other, and may be roughly
divided into two heads, those which, like the poor's rate, part of
the watching rate, the county and borough rates, are referable
to the government and social administration of the country, and
those which, like the general district, sewerage, town improvements, and drainage rates generally, are raised for purposes in
which the owners, and the ratepayers as well, presumably have a
beneficial interest, in the shape either of sanitary or other improvement. The general division, as well as the recent increase, is
described in Mr. Goschen's report, as follows :—

" To sum up this part of my subject, it should be remembered
" that, on the broadest historical survey, there has been, since 1841,
" an increase of 8,000,000l. in local burdens, of which—

£	
2,000,000	are due to poor law expenditure, which excess for the present I will assume to be partly rural, partly urban.
5,500,000	are due to new rates, for the most part imposed since 1840, of which 5,000,000l. are due to town rates, and only 500,000l. to county police.
500,000	are due to an increase in highway rates and county rates, and miscellaneous expenditure, of which the main portion falls on rural districts.

8,000,000

" Thus,

£	
5,000,000	would fall on towns.
1,000,000	,, rural districts.
2,000,000	on poor law unions, which for the present may be considered as partly rural and partly urban. [In a later portion of my report I deal with the distribution of this increase.]

" Of the total rates of 16,500,000l. (in round numbers) now
" spent by local authorities, the following is a broad analysis:—

£		
5,000,000,	or 30·0 per cent.,	are exclusively urban rates.
3,000,000,	,, 18·5 ,,	being county and highway rates, are exclusively rural.
8,000,000,	,, 48·5 ,,	being poor law expenditure; and,
500,000,	,, 3·0 ,,	being miscellaneous rates, are partly urban and partly rural.

16,500,000	100·0 "*

---

* " Report on Local Taxation, No. 470, 1870."

The authorities by whom the local rates are levied and expended, differ no less widely than the purposes for which they are raised. The rates may, for this purpose, be again divided into two classes :
I. Those which are levied by one authority and expended by another.
II. Those which are levied and expended by the same authority.

It will be observed that the principal part of the local taxation of the country falls within the first division. The administration of the amounts levied is thus separated in great measure from those who contribute the sums raised.* Nor is this deficiency of control in the local powers supplemented in any real degree by the central authority. Instead, this naturally feeble control is further greatly diminished in power by the manner in which the governing bodies themselves are constituted. The boards of guardians for the poor and highway boards, consist partly of *ex officio*, partly of elected members. The numbers in 1870 were :—

	Elected Guardians.	*Ex Officio* Guardians.	Total.
England	19,098	6,426	25,524
Wales	1,427	668	2,095
Total	20,525	7,094	27,619

The county rates are entirely assessed and administered by *ex officio* authority, in the appointment of which the ratepayers have absolutely no authority whatever.†

The following remarks of the Sanitary Commissioners' Report of 1870, refer to some of the evils which result from this confusion of authorities :—

" Local government is greatly impeded and wasted by the want " of coincidence of the several areas of its various jurisdictions. " The petty sessional divisions, poor law unions, and highway

---

* " The existing inspecting power of the Local Government Act Office is utterly " inadequate even to the present requirements—being, according to Mr. Taylor's " estimate, about half what is necessary—and yet in the opinion of our most com- " petent witnesses, effective inspection is the key to the working of the whole " machinery. We deprecate the maintenance of parallel inspectorates of sanitary " and poor law administration under the same chief minister, not only on the ground " of waste of powers, but still more of probable conflict. We agree generally in " Mr. Redgrave's opinion that there should be one staff for enforcing all regulations " bearing on the health of the people."—" Report of the Sanitary Commission, " 1870," p. 33.

† Table N shows that in the year 1867 the rates thus levied amounted in England to 1,343,065*l.* per annum, in Wales to 105,465*l.*, while debts had been incurred amounting to 2,379,899*l.* in England, and 204,092*l.* in Wales. This table likewise shows the increasing character of the sums thus administered during the period 1856-67.

" districts being generally different, a corresponding difference
" occurs in much that appertains to the administration. Instead of
" one superior clerk for all these, one single collection of rates, one
" set of officers for inspections, and a uniform system and concert of
" plans, and of their enforcement, each must have it own machinery,
" frequently in conflict or in duplicate, as the areas happen to be
" partly the same, partly different; and there can neither be com-
" bined efficiency nor general economy."—" Report of the Sanitary
" Commissioners, 1870," p. 21.

The manner in which the elected authorities are appointed
differs very greatly in almost every point. It may be added that
the mode of voting for the different governing local authorities is
also not uniform. Thus the guardians of the poor in municipal
boroughs are elected by a voting paper left at each house, to be
initialled and signed by the voter. These voting papers are gathered
in by an authorised collector, and the clerk to the guardians makes
the return. In the case of town councils, a voting paper is likewise left; this the voter has not only to sign, but to deliver in
person at the appointed polling place for the ward, the alderman
presiding over the poll. As modes of election in this country
appear likely to be modified shortly, it may be only needful to mention here, that the plan adopted in the election of guardians, though
it protects the voter from the influence and intimidation which may
possibly be brought to bear on the timid or needy at the polling
place, or on the way thither, is nevertheless open to the objection
that, in the case of the poorer and more illiterate voters, and
especially of those who sign by a mark, and require the presence of a
witness; that witness, who will probably be the collector of the
voting papers, may exercise an undue influence, and, if an employé
of the existing board, will always be liable to the imputation,
whether deserved or not, of thus endeavouring to promote the
interests of his employers. The existing mode of voting for town
councillors is, however, open to greater objections than these, and
leads in many cases frequently, it is to be feared usually, to treating,
bribery, and many of the evils attendant on the elections for Members
of Parliament.

The only point of uniformity of procedure is that the rate in
almost every instance, is paid by the occupier in England. A portion
of the tax, however, beyond doubt, is ultimately paid by the owner.
In very few cases, however, has the owner, as such, any power in
controlling the expenditure of the taxation on his property. The
subject is further complicated by the fact that in many instances
the ownership is divided. Thus a house is frequently owned by a
leaseholder for a term of years. The leaseholder pays a ground-
rent to the landowner, and receives a rent for the house from a

tenant. This is but one instance of the difficulties in the complicated questions which arise from the variety in procedure, joined
with variety in tenure.

As mentioned above, the purposes for which rates are levied are
broadly divided into two heads:—

I. Government and social administration.

II. Improvement and sanitary purposes.

The first head includes the expenditure under the poor law,
" the largest branch of expenditure for local purposes of all local
" burdens. In this item there has been, broadly speaking, a con-
" siderable increase. The fluctuations, indeed, have been so great,
" that the most contrary conclusions might be drawn by statis-
" ticians if they were permitted to select single years for com-
" parison. The fair mode of dealing with this expenditure is to
" take averages over certain periods, long enough to afford time for
" the operation of exceptional causes to be counterbalanced by the
" effects of several ordinary years.

" The result of taking averages over the last fifty years, in
" decennial periods, is as follows:—

			£
Average yearly expenditure for poor relief,	1819-29	....	6,300,000
"	"	'29-39	....	5,700,000
"	"	'39-49	....	5,200,000
"	"	'49-59	....	5,500,000
"	"	'59-69	....	6,500,000

" These figures show that this branch of expenditure has risen
" from the lowest average, 5,200,000*l.*, to the highest average,
" 6,500,000*l.*, showing an increase of 1,300,000*l.* But it may fairly
" be said that, looking to the last five years, the average of the last
" ten years affords an insufficient notion of the present charge. The
" figures should be considered more in detail. It is to be remarked
" that—

				£
The lowest figure during the whole period was, in 1837	....	4,050,000
" highest " " '69	....	7,700,000
The highest figure in the first ten years of the series was, in 1820	....	7,330,000
"	second	"	'30	....	6,830,000
"	third	"	'48	....	6,180,000
"	fourth	"	'56	....	6,000,000
"	fifth	"	'69	....	7,700,000

" It thus appears that the average increase in the last decade
" has been 1,300,000*l.* over the *lowest* decade in the last fifty years.
" This sum represents the average annual disadvantage to which
" rateable property has been subjected during the last ten years in
" respect of expenditure for the relief of the poor, as compared with
" the most favourable decade in the century, irrespective of the

" increase in the value of rateable property, and of the parts of the
" country where the increase has taken place. But let it be assumed
" that the expenditure for the last year has been normal, and that
" 7,700,000l. represents the probable cost of the relief of the poor
" for future years; let this amount then be compared with the
" average expenditure not of the heavy years between 1812 and
" 1819, but of the forty years, 1820-60, for which the average
" expenditure was between 5,700,000l. and 5,800,000l.; and the
" present excess is, therefore, a little under 2,000,000l."—" Report
" on Local Taxation, 1870."

Though the working of the poor law in England has been open
to great objections, yet the parochial system, defective as it is, has
done much to counteract many of the abuses of the administration
of that law. The influence of the parochial system in this respect,
has been clearly and briefly stated by the late Mr. Ricardo, in
words which are still very applicable to the present time, notwithstanding the many alterations which have taken place since they
were written:—

" The present mode of collecting and applying the fund for the
" support of the poor has served to mitigate its pernicious effects.
" Each parish raises a separate fund for the support of its own
" poor. Hence it becomes an object of more interest and more
" practicability to keep the rates low, than if one general fund was
" raised for the relief of the whole kingdom. A parish is much
" more interested in an economical collection of the rate, and a
" sparing distribution of relief, when the whole saving will be for
" its own benefit, than if hundreds of parishes were to partake of
" it."—" Ricardo's Principles of Political Economy." First edition,
p. 113.

The operation of the English law of settlement, combined with
this strong local interest in the amount of poor rates levied in each
parish, led, however, to some abuses, by means of which certain
parishes, principally in the hands of individuals, avoided their due
share of the general burden. Recent legislation has mitigated
some of these abuses. One very important alteration was effected
in the law by the passing of the Union Chargeability Act, 28 and
29 Vict., cap. 70. " Under the provisions of this Act some parishes
" which, from peculiar circumstances, had escaped the burden of
" the relief of the poor, and extra-parochial places which had
" hitherto been exempted from it, will incur some additional pecu-
" niary liability, but there can be little doubt that all places com-
" prised in one union, and having such mutual interests as their
" vicinity to each other must create, may properly be required to
" bear in common the relief of those who become destitute within its
" limits; and we trust that, whilst it will lead to an improved and

c

" uniform management of the poor, it will also be found no less
" beneficial to the labouring class and the owner and occupier of
" property."—"Eighteenth Report of the Poor Law Board,"
p. 21.

The effect of this Act is thus described in a circular issued by
the Poor Law Board, 28th February, 1866, calling the attention of
boards of guardians to the changes to take effect from the 25th of
the next month :—" From and after that day the separate parochial
" chargeability of the poor in the union will cease. Thenceforth all
" the cost of the relief of the poor and the expenses of the burial of
" the dead under the direction of the guardians or their officers,
" vaccination fees, and registration fees, and expenses are to be
" charged to the common fund of the union."—" Nineteenth Annual
" Report," p. 34. The Metropolitan Poor Act of 1867, creating
a metropolitan common poor fund, is an enactment similar in
character to the preceding adjusted to metropolitan requirements.*
The expenses chargeable to this fund, and the area of the operation
of the Act, are stated below. These alterations are designed to
mitigate some of the most oppressive effects of the incidence of
the poor's rate in particular localities.

The above-named alterations are, as stated, designed to effect
a more equitable mode of contribution; meanwhile the efforts of
the late President of the Poor Law Board (Mr. Goschen) have been
continually directed to measures intended to diminish the general
charge by judicious management.† The arrangements for separate
schools for pauper children in certain places; the endeavour to
organise a well-regulated system of boarding-out such children—
both appear well digested plans for endeavouring to diminish the
great amount of hereditary pauperism. The establishment of a
training ship for orphan boys, has been also referred to as likely to
promise a " satisfactory outlet " for such children.—(See "Twenty-
" second Report of Poor Law Board," LV.) But notwithstanding
these and other similar plans, a vast amount of pauperism will
remain, at least for many years, a charge on the energies of the
country.

When the present system of poor relief was first established in
England, and for many years subsequently, it is probable that the
weight of the tax was borne by the land of the country. The
original intention of the legislation of Elizabeth was to combine
voluntary with compulsory contribution; where the former method
failed, " it seems to have been thought that the tax could be laid on
" the occupier without affecting the owner of the land."—" Report
" on Local Taxation, 1843," p. 33.

* *Vide* Appendix, No. V.

† Some remarks by Mr. McCulloch are given, Appendix IV, on the Scotch
system.

But since that period a vast alteration has taken place in the constitution of the property of the country, and consequently in the incidence of the tax.

This point, namely the progressive increase of the value of real property other than land, forms so important an element in the consideration of this portion of the question that a Table (M) has been added to illustrate the subject, by showing that the alteration in the character of "realty," is not the result of any casual circumstances, but of the tendency of affairs in the country generally. This table extends over a period earlier in date than that proposed for this immediate inquiry, but the additional illustration it affords, will, it is hoped, be a sufficient justification for its introduction. By its aid it becomes clear that "lands and other descriptions of real property," have, broadly speaking, in the course of half a century, changed places in regard to value; and likewise consequently in the amount of contribution to this form of direct taxation. Table M likewise shows the progressive character of the increase, and, to use the words of Mr. Purdy we may say that in 1864-65 as against 1851-52, that 10·3 per cent. has passed from the land and gone upon other assessable property. Land would appear now liable to bear rather more than one-third of any burden laid upon real property generally; and real property other than land rather less than two-thirds. Mr. Goschen's calculations, comparing the years 1814, 1843, and 1868, support this statement :—

" If we take, in the first place, the variations in the proportions
" of the value of lands to houses and other property, and the
" variations in the amount of the burdens borne by each respec-
" tively, we find more evidence bearing upon the increase in value
" than upon the proportionate shares borne by each at different
" periods; but as regards *value*, the materials exist for the year
" 1814, and for the whole series of years between 1843 and 1868.

" In the year 1814 the total annual value was 53,495,000*l*., dis-
" tributed as follows :—

	£
Lands	37,063,000
Houses	14,895,000
Railways	—
Other property	1,537,000

" In 1843 the total value was 85,803,000*l*., distributed as
" follows :—

	£
Lands	42,128,000
Houses	35,556,000
Railways	2,418,000
Other property	5,701,000
Total	85,803,000

" In 1868 the total value was 143,873,000l., distributed as
follows :—

£

Lands	47,767,000
Houses...	68,013,000
Railways (Schedule D)	15,980,000
Other property (Schedule D)	12,113,000
Total	143,873,000

" The percentages of the various classes of property to the total
" value of real property, are worked out with the following
" results :—

	1814.	1843.	1868.
Lands	69·28	49·10	33·20
Houses...........................	27·84	41·44	47·27
Railways.......................	—	2·82	11·11
Other property	2·88	6·64	8·42
	100·00	100·00	100·00

£   £

Land increased in value, between 1814 and 1843, 13·66 per cent., viz., from } 37,063,000 to 42,127,000

Houses increased in value between 1814 and 1843, 138·71 per cent., viz., from } 14,895,000 ,, 35,556,000

Other property, including railways, increased in value, between 1814 and 1843, 428·18 per cent., viz., from } 1,537,000 ,, 8,118,000

The total increase of all property between the same two years was 60·39 per
cent.

" Taking the comparison between 1814 and 1868, the facts are
" these :—

£   £

Land increased, between 1814 and 1843, 28·88 per cent., viz., from } 37,063,000 to 47,766,000

Houses increased, between 1814 and 1843, 356·61 per cent., viz., from } 14,895,000 ,, 68,022,000

Other property, including railways, increased between 1814 and 1843, 1,727·72 per cent., viz., from } 1,537,000 ,, 28,092,000

The total increase of all property between the same two years being
168·94 per cent.

" It appears from the foregoing figures that a complete revolu-
" tion has taken place in the relative position of lands and other
" classes of property as contributors to local taxation. While in
" 1814, lands, speaking broadly, represented 70 per cent. of the total
" value of real property, they now represent only 33 per cent., or
" less than half of the previous percentage ; houses, which in 1814

" contributed only 27·84 per cent., or little more than one-quarter of
" the value of real property, now represent 47·27, or nearly one-half;
" while railways and other property, which in 1814 contributed only
" 2·88 to the whole, now together contribute 19·53.

"The scope of these facts in their effect upon the incidence of
" local taxation will not escape attention. It will be seen that
" though the increase in the value of lands has been decided and
" progressive, it has been far outstripped by the progress of other
" kinds of property. If the amount of taxation had remained the
" same, it is clear that a great portion of the burden originally borne
" by lands would have been shifted on to other classes of property ;
" but the aggregate amount of taxation has increased. Has that
" portion of it which falls on lands increased in a greater proportion
" than the 28·88 per cent. which lands themselves have increased in
" value ? The analysis already given as to the increase in local
" burdens, and the particular rates in which the increase is most
" marked, shows that it has not. Irrespective of the new rates,
" there has been a marked decrease in the average rate in the pound,
" and the increased proportion of the new rates, being exclusively
" urban, has fallen not on land, but on houses and other property.
" Materials exist for testing conclusively the truth of this view, even
" if the statement showing the growth of new rates in towns did not
" prove it."—" Report on Local Taxation, 1870," p. 19.

With regard to the amount of poor's rates raised in the agricultural districts, the effect of a system of organised poor relief like that
of England and Wales on the wage-earning classes, must not be lost
sight of. There is little doubt but that it does to a certain extent
cheapen labour. Mr. Purdy considers that "English poor rates largely
" supplement wages, and consumers thereby gain some temporary but
" in its consequences more than doubtful benefit."* According to
Mr. Thorold Rogers : " Economically considered, a poor rate is an
" insurance of the labourer's life and health. It maintains him
" in old age, assists him in sickness, protects him when labouring
" under mental disease, and supplies him with the services of a
" highly skilled person in the shape of a medical officer. Now it is
" plain that at the existing rate of agricultural wages, the farm
" labourer, and, to some extent the artisan, could hardly supply
" these services for himself. A poor rate, then, is a rate in aid of
" wages, under which wages are supplemented, and, therefore, the
" prime cost of labour is diminished. The poor rate, then, is not
" wholly loss. It cheapens labour, and so increases rent. Take it
" away, and a considerable portion of that which the landowners
" might receive in the shape of an increased rent, due to a diminished

* *Vide* Mr. Purdy on the Pressure of Taxation on Real Property.—*Statistical
Society's Journal*, vol. xxxii, p. 319.

" outlay for the maintenance of the poor, would be re-assumed by
" the farmer in consequence of the exalted cost at which labour would
" be procurable. It is a notorious fact, that where wages are low,
" poor rates are high."*

Table O gives the rate of wages in those English counties in
which poor rates are relatively the highest and lowest, and bears
out this statement to a certain extent. There are also other large
employers of labour in this country beside farmers; and manufac-
turers of all descriptions participate in this "doubtful benefit" in
a somewhat similar manner, and in the proportion which the cost
of labour bears to the total expense of production. As in many
descriptions of manufactures the expenditure on labour bears a
large ratio to the total cost, the question so far does not apply less
to the urban than to the rural employer. The difference in the
wages paid and the difference in the social position of the two
classes of workpeople must not, however, be lost sight of. It is
probable that the classes who, in proportion to their taxation to the
poor's rate, gain the least collateral advantage from it, are the pro-
fessional, the non-productive, and the small shopkeepers. Although
from its nature statistical proof is impossible, yet it does not admit
of a doubt that, in many instances, the poor's rates press very
heavily on many of the classes but one remove from pauperism.
It is desirable that the late Mr. Ricardo's thoughtful remarks on
the subject should not be forgotten.†

---

* *Vide* Professor J. E. T. Rogers on the Incidence of Local Taxation.—
Statistical Society's Journal, vol. xxxiii, pp. 250 and 251.

† " No scheme for the amendment of the poor laws merits the least attention,
" which has not their abolition for its ultimate object ; and he is the best friend
" to the poor and to the cause of humanity, who can point out how this end can
" be attained with the most security, and at the same time with the least violence.
" It is not by raising in any manner different from the present, the fund from
" which the poor are supported, that the evil can be mitigated. It would not only
" be no improvement, but it would be an aggravation of the distress which we wish
" to see removed, if the fund were increased in amount, or were levied according to
" some late proposals, as a general fund from the country at large. The present
" mode of its collection and application has served to mitigate its pernicious effects.
" Each parish raises a separate fund for the support of its own poor. Hence it
" becomes an object of more interest and more practicability to keep the rates low,
" than if one general fund were raised for the relief of the poor of the whole
" kingdom. A parish is much more interested in an economical collection of the
" rate, and a sparing distribution of relief, when the whole saving will be for its
" own benefit, than if hundreds of other parishes were to partake of it.
" It is to this cause that we must ascribe the fact of the poor laws not having
" yet absorbed all the net revenue of the country ; it is to the rigour with which
" they are applied, that we are indebted for their not having become overwhelmingly
" oppressive. If by law every human being wanting support could be sure to
" obtain it, and obtain it in such a degree as to make life tolerably comfortable,
" theory would lead us to expect that all other taxes together would be light com-
" pared with the single one of poor rates. The principle of gravitation is not more
" certain than the tendency of such laws to change wealth and power into misery and

More detail has been entered into with regard to the poor rate
than will be needful in the case of any other individual local charge.
This has been considered desirable on account of the large amount
of levy required, the great difficulties of the subject, and because
this portion of taxation is almost the only one in which it appears
probable that any great diminution of the charge necessarily
incurred can be obtained from judicious legislation on the subject
itself. A careful management of the poor law may, it is hoped,
diminish pauperism and the expenses incident thereon. Other local
requirements appear likely to increase, rather than to diminish, in
charge. Improvements in administration may, it is hoped, tend to
economy. Some hints for improvements are suggested further on,
but the poor law administration in all its divisions presents the
widest field.

                                                     £

1. The amount levied for poor relief in 1868 was 7,825,592
2. County, hundred, borough, and police rate—
    a. Contributed from poor rate £2,462,922
    b. Levied separately............................ 493,285
                           ——— 2,956,207
3. Highway rate—
    a. Contributed from poor rate 621,436
    b. Levied separately............................ 916,779
                           ——— 1,538,215
4. Church rates 217,482
5. Lighting and watching rate* 79,393

"The chief expenditure which the county rates are intended to
"cover may, as a rule, be taken to be that in respect of county
"bridges, gaols, and shirehalls, county lunatic asylums, and county
"police; but there are many other objects which, in the aggregate,
"form a large portion of the entire expenditure.

"The hundred rate is, as its name shows, limited to hundreds,
"and it is now only leviable for the purpose of making good
"damage to property in cases of riot.

"The borough rates are levied in municipal cities and boroughs
"in which the county justices have either no jurisdiction or a

"weakness; to call away the exertions of labour from every object, except that of
"providing mere subsistence; to confound all intellectual distinction; to busy
"the mind continually in supplying the body's wants; until at last all
"classes should be infected with the plague of universal poverty. Happily these
"laws have been in operation during a period of progressive prosperity, when the
"funds for the maintenance of labour have regularly increased, and when an
"increase of population would naturally be called for. But if our progress should
"become more slow ; if we should attain the stationary state, from which I trust
"we are yet far distant, then will the pernicious nature of these laws become more
"manifest and alarming ; and then, too, will their removal be obstructed by many
"additional difficulties."—"Ricardo's Principles of Political Economy." Second
edition, pp. 58 and 59.
   * "Return on Local Taxation, No. 430, 1870," p. iv.

" partial jurisdiction only; and they embrace, to a great extent,
" similar objects to those provided for by the county rates."—
" Report of Select Committee (353), Local Taxation, 1870,"
p. xi.

These complete the rates raised for the purposes of government
and social administration. Some questions have arisen on some of
these rates: whether police expenses, the administration of justice,
gaols, and some other similar charges do not more properly belong
to imperial than to local legislation. These points will be considered further on.

The rates raised for purposes of health and local improvements
are, speaking generally :—

	£
6. Improvement Commissioners.......................................	410,105
7. General district rates	1,683,702
8. „ and lighting rates in the metropolis	981,140
9. Rates under courts or Commissioners of Sewers } (including drainage and embankment rates)........ }	714,734
10. Rates of other kinds—	
a. Contributed from poor rates............ £152,076	
b. Levied separately 224,574	
	376,650
Total (with the amounts 1 to 5 in pre- } ceding table) * .... }	16,783,220

" The general district rate, which is levied by local boards under
" the Public Health and Local Government Acts, is applied in
" defraying the expenses of making and maintaining sewers and
" drains, public streets and highways, and various works of town
" improvement ; and the rates levied by the Metropolitan Board of
" Works and the several district boards in the metropolis are for
" the most part applied towards similar objects.

" The sewers rate is not, as its name would seem to imply,
" levied for the purposes of sewerage, as that term is now under-
" stood, but for works of drainage and embankment."—"Report
" of Select Committee on Local Taxation (353), 1870," p. xi.

As stated by Mr. Purdy, in his valuable paper on the Pressure
of Taxation on Real Property, in the *Statistical Society's Journal*,
vol. xxxii, p. 319 :—"Expenditure upon the maintenance and
" repair of roads and bridges, upon the drainage and embankment
" of marsh lands, upon the sewerage, paving and lighting of towns,
" and upon many other services performed by improvement com-
" missioners, as well as the sanitary measures undertaken by boards
" of health, are operations signally beneficial to rateable property.

" So far, therefore, as the property is judiciously assessed, and

---

* " Return on Local Taxation, No. 430, 1870," p. iv.

" the proceeds honestly and intelligently administered for these
" purposes, the local rate is a good investment, for which no
" enlightened owner will manifest an ignorant. impatience of
" taxation. The imperial taxes and the other portion of the local
" rates stand in a very different category."

This branch of the question has also been the subject of much
inquiry, principally as to the point whether such expenses as are
incurred for the improvement of property are in fairness chargeable
on the occupier, when the owner is the person principally benefited.
Some remarks on this question will be found at p. 65.

III.—*Local Administration.*

Having thus given an outline of the subject, of the amounts
annually raised, and of the purposes for which the taxation is levied,
it is desirable to enter more into detail on some of the principal
points concerned.

Economy in administration is scarcely possible where conflicting
jurisdictions and needless multiplications of offices exist.   The
number of officers employed in the business of the local taxation
of the country is very large indeed.   No recent and complete
returns exist of the number of these officers.   The Report of the
Poor Law Commissioners on Local Taxation in 1843, gives a statement as to their numbers at that time.   It contains a list of officers
engaged " in assessing, collecting, levying, keeping, expending, and
" auditing of local rates and taxes."   This list occupies twenty-five
pages of small octavo size.   It is stated that " the number of
" officers engaged in collecting, levying, and keeping of local rates
" and taxes, and in accounting for them, and in auditing accounts
" is, as the law provides for them, much more considerable than is
" usually supposed.   There are no less than fifty-four different
" species of officers ; of each species there are often several indi-
" viduals of each district.   Their total number cannot be ascer-
" tained from any existing documents ; but those in office simul-
" taneously cannot be less than 180,000, of whom by far the larger
" portion are annual officers, to be succeeded every year by a like
" number of new officers.   Their districts and their modes of
" appointment vary greatly."—" Report on Local Taxation, 1843,"
p. 121.

Some of the officers therein named have been displaced from
power by more recent legislation.   The numbers of others have
been curtailed.   But there has been extension more than compensating in other directions.

Since the date of the report of 1843, no fewer than eleven rates
have been created.

These are :—

> *Burial Board Rate.*
> *Public Library and Museum Rate.*
> *General District Rate.*
> *Sewerage Rate.*
> *Parish Improvement Rate.*
> *Animals Contagious Diseases Rate.*
> *Borough Lunatic Asylum Rate.*
> *Borough Library and Museum Rate.* -
> *Borough Baths and Washhouses Rate.*
> *Borough Improvement Rate.*
> *Borough Burial Board Rate.*

A "special district rate" also is still leviable under the Public Health Act in certain cases.* Several of these rates are extensions of the previously existing system and are worked by the administration in use before. Others, as the library and museum rates, baths and washouses rates, mark requirements more keenly felt of late years, and call into action a different staff of officials. It is thus probable that not only the fifty-four species of officers engaged in administering and levying local rates, but also the number of 180,000 individual officers so engaged in 1843 must be largely augmented.†

The memorandum drawn up by Mr. Coode, Assistant Secretary to the Commission, may be regarded generally applicable to the state of matters still existing, and is given in the Appendix to the Report of 1843.

The want of system in the local administration of Great Britain appears marvellous to those foreigners who have inquired into it, and is well given in the following words of M. de Parieu :—

" M. de Mohl, dans son savant ouvrage allemand sur l'histoire " et la littérature des sciences politiques, apprécie avec des termes

---

* " In the year 1858, the Local Government Act, which is to be construed with " the Public Health Act of 1848, as one Act, was passed, and took effect in all " places where that Act was in force at the time of its passing, and the two " together constitute the principal sanitary legislation now on the statute book.
" The Local Government Act, 1858, amended the Public Health Act of 1848, " as to the constitution and powers of local boards of health in towns or populous " districts in England and Wales, excepting the metropolis. It handed over to the " Home Secretary the few remaining functions of the discontinued general board " for the purposes of sanctions, provisional orders, and appeals, and the Local " Government Act Office was made a sub-department of the Home Office for the " execution of the Act, and for the central superintendence and assistance of all " local boards."—" Report of the Sanitary Commissioners, 1871," p. 9.

† In reference to this subject it may be observed that the 180,000 officers, " 17,716 guardians for unions, omitting *ex officio* guardians," are enumerated. The corresponding number for 1870 is 20,525; making, with 7,094 *ex officio* guardians, 27,619 in all. Under this head alone, therefore, there is a very considerable increase.

" fort sévères le système des taxes locales de l'Empire Britannique,
" qu'il paraît avoir étudié surtout au point de vue administratif :

" Il y a dans ce système de taxes accessoires, dit-il, un effroyable
" chaos de mauvaises mesures et de désordre ; c'est une preuve
" nouvelle de la fausseté du principe fondamental de la legislation
" Anglaise, qui consiste à pourvoir à chacque cas isolé, en negligeant
" toutes les pensées et les dispositions générales et puissantes.
" C'est ainsi qu'on est arrivé à ce resultat, en realité barbare,
" d'établir une taxe locale spéciale pour chaque nature de dépense
" locale. Ces taxes sont souvent si insignificantes que le contingent
" de chaque contribuable ne peut guère être saisi, et que les frais de
" perception dépassent le montant de la taxe elle-même. Ainsi en
" est-il de la *dead burial rate*, pour l'inhumation des cadavres laissés
" sur le rivage. Dans beaucoup de cas, le contre-sens est si grand
" que les juges de paix n'exécutent pas littéralement la loi, mais
" prélèvent la somme nécessaire sur une autre taxe, et ordinaire-
" ment sur la taxe des pauvres.

" Qui pourrait croire que dans l'Angleterre et la pays de Galles,
" il n'y a pas moins de vingt-quatres diverses taxes locales qui sont
" imposées et levées d'après les dispositions de 173 lois différentes
" par 18,000 fonctionaires le plus souvent gratuits ? Que, pour
" plusieurs de ces taxes, un mode de perception très-prodigue, une
" supputation incertaine, une comptabilité défectueuse, accompag-
" nent un luxe exagéré dans les dépenses que l'impôt doit couvrir ?
" Qu'il en est de même en Ecosse et en Irelande, bien qu'à un
" moindre dégre ? Qu'enfin il se lève de cette manière environ
" 12 millions de livres sterling, soit 300 millions de francs."—From
" Traité des Impôts, par M. Esquirou de Parieu," vol iv, pp. 193
and 194.

The remedies recommended in 1843 have unfortunately not
been adopted, although the inconveniences then felt have by no
means diminished in the interim.

" Thus, putting out of consideration the taxes and various modi-
" fications of detail created by local and special customs, or by local
" Acts of Parliament, there is found in the common law and the
" general statutes authority to impose and levy, for about two
" hundred various and imperfectly defined purposes, at least twenty-
" four different local taxes, a large portion of which would, if the
" law were to be carried into effect according to its intention, be
" levied separately and distinctly in every district, some of them
" permanently, some occasionally, and many of them for the pur-
" pose of raising sums of money quite insignificant in amount. The
" definitions of the persons on whom the taxes are imposed often
" vary without apparent cause, and sometimes are inconsistent with
" what is generally supposed to have been the intention of the

" legislature; the definitions of the property in respect of which
" the taxes are assessed being still more various, and involved in
" still more frequent difficulty. Some of these taxes admit, in
" the process of their imposition and enforcement, of a great
" latitude of discretion, others of none; some of them are sub-
" jected to no legal check or remedy, some to very cumbrous or
" expensive ones, while, with regard to others, complainants are
" embarrassed by the multitude of the facilities for litigation.
" Again, other taxes are incapable of being levied if resisted; others
" are only to be levied with great difficulty and cost; others
" enforced by most stringent, vexatious, and extraordinary means.
" In some cases there is entirely wanting the protection involved in
" the accountability of the officers who impose the tax, or collect it,
" or disburse it; in some there are partial protections, but there is
" not one case of an efficient protection. The execution of this
" multifarious and discordant mass of law is confided to a body of
" not less 150,000 officers, the greater part of whom are unpaid,
" little responsible, and changed annually, and who are nevertheless
" entrusted with the imposition of not less than twelve millions of
" pounds sterling in England and Wales, and with the application
" of this vast amount of money. Such great temptations and
" opportunities for abuse cannot exist without a great amount of
" illegality and extravagance."—" Report of the Poor Law Commis-
" sioners on Local Taxation, 1843," p. 145.

IV.—*Macclesfield as an Example of Local Administration.*

The different descriptions of local officers correspond with
different systems of administration. There are generally at least
three different governing bodies in each municipal borough in
England and Wales, viz. :—

The board of guardians for the poor,
The town council,
The local board of health.

The number of the last is about 674, not including the vestries and
district boards of the metropolis.* The boards of guardians are
collected into union boards; the area of the union in which the
borough is situated being very rarely conterminous with that of the
borough. The town council, though the same body as the local
board of health, yet acts with different functions. The evidence of
Mr. John May before the Select Committee of 1870, sets forth these
various jurisdictions in a remarkably clear way. Mr. May describes
himself as clerk to the guardians of the Macclesfield union, likewise

---

* *Vide* Mr. Tom Taylor's evidence before the Committee of the House of
Commons, 1870, par. 419.

as clerk to the local board of health, while his partner is town clerk of the borough of Macclesfield. The local board of health and the town council are the same body, but as a matter of convenience they meet separately and on different days, because their functions are different. The town council attends to all matters of police, and appoints various committees, finance committees, general purpose committees and others, levies a borough rate, manages the waterworks, and levies a water rate. The local board manages the gasworks, levies rates for the maintenance of the roads, and for all sanitary purposes, and administers those funds. The town council and the local board keep different sets of accounts, in different sets of books, and have different balances at their bankers. They raise different rates at different times, and have different collectors. These collectors each collect two different principal rates. The borough rate levied by the council is paid out of the poor rates in the township of Macclesfield; these two rates being collected at the same time by one officer. A cemetery rate and a contribution to the county lunatic asylum, are likewise paid out of the poor rate. The board of health levy a general district rate, and a lighting rate. These two rates are kept separate, but are collected at the same time. The general district rate is described as being 1s. 6d. in the pound; the lighting rate is 6d. in the pound. These rates are kept distinct in the ledger. The general district rate is levied like all rates under the Public Health Act, with an exemption of 75 per cent. in favour of market gardens, land, railways, and so forth. The borough rate is levied with the poor rate, and on the basis of the poor rate, in which these exemptions do not exist.

"Accordingly the borough rate is levied upon all alike, whereas" the general district rate is levied in a different proportion;" while although the purposes of the two rates are not identical, they are "similar for the general advantage of the town."

A different arrangement for compounding for small properties exists for the poor and the general district rates. For the former the Assessed Rates Act has been put in force, in which the limit is 8l. and under. For the latter the limit is 10l. and under. Different allowances are made in the two rates. Thus the owner of the same house is taxed in a different way with different deductions for those two different rates.

The "borough" and the "township" are not conterminous, the "borough" boundary cutting the "township" into two parts. The part of the "township" outside the "borough" pays the county rate, the part inside the borough pays "county rate "exclusive of police," and borough rate as well, the borough rate being a charge for police only. Though the borough, as mentioned above, contributes to the building of the county lunatic asylum, it has no control over that expenditure except through the county justices resident in the borough, who, however, vote as county justices, and not as the representatives of the borough. The rates for the borough are materially assisted by the surplus tolls on the River Weaver; but the ratepayers of the borough, as such, have no control over the navigation or the expenses. In the modes of electing the governing bodies of the borough a similar diversity prevails as in the proceedings relating to local taxation. There are three elections which occur annually in the borough: the municipal election, the election for guardians, and the proceedings in the vestry in the case of overseers. All these three elections are conducted with different qualifications, on what may be termed a different register for each. Besides, there is the election of borough members, also on a different register. Thus, there are four registers, the conditions of voting being different in each case, the owners of property having a different position in all. For the vestry and the election of guardians, the rate book is the register. For the election of borough members and of the town council, separate registers are made out, with a repetition of expenses in the preparation of those registers.*

This description of the local government of Macclesfield is taken from the evidence given by Mr. May before the Select Committee of the House of Commons.† It is not given here as being exceptional in any way, but as a fair typical example.

V.—*Existing System of Collection.*

Some incidental but important points, were reserved for further consideration in the outline of the main question given above. Among these are the objections which have been made to the manner in which the existing local taxation is raised, and to defraying certain charges from local funds.

There are similar diversities in the way of appointment of local officers in every municipal borough, as those which exist in Macclesfield, and greater diversities of rates and even a larger number exists in other places. A greater number of rates were stated before the Committee to be levied in Leeds. This also appears to be the case in Liverpool. An unpublished return of local taxation

---

* *Variety of Areas for Rating Purposes*—
"4703. It would appear, would it not, that there are a variety of areas in "the county of Lancaster for rating purposes?—That is so. There are about "thirty-five for county rate purposes, the rates in each case being dissimilar."— *Mr. J. Grant,* "Report on Local Taxation, 1870."

† *Vide* evidence of Mr. John May before the Select Committee of the House of Commons, par. 5235—5472.

in certain parishes in Lancashire and Cheshire, made by the clerk to the guardians of Liverpool, and kindly supplied by him to the author, shows not only that a larger number of rates is frequently made, but that greater diversities in the mode of assessment prevail. At Salford, with respect to the latter point, a remark was made in reply to inquiries instituted by the author, "there appears " to be no fixed rule."

The mode of collecting the different rates levied throughout the country, being obviously extremely deficient in method, it may be desirable to refer, by way of contrast, to the system followed by the Commissioners of Inland Revenue.

This may be briefly described as a division of the country into large districts, carefully adapted to local requirements. Every district possessing a complete and well-organised body of trained officers; working each in his own department, under the constant supervision of a superior officer.

General View of the Excise Surveying Department.

" The excise duties of inland revenue are charged and collected " by a number of commissioned officers, who form what is called " the Excise Surveying Establishment. For the convenience of " business each part of the United Kingdom is divided into several " large sections, technically termed collections. A collection is " made to consist as far as possible, of a certain number of whole " parishes or townships, and is proportioned to the number of " traders in different localities or the magnitude of their operations. " Usually a collection takes its title from the name of some large " city or town, prescribed as the residence of the principal officer.

" Each collection is presided over by a collector, an officer who " holds the highest local rank in the surveying department.

" Collections are subdivided into districts, and these again into " divisions (or footwalks) and rides.

" The officer in charge of a district is called a supervisor, and is " next in rank below a collector. The fixed surveying officers are " of two classes—1. Division officers. 2. Ride officers.

" In Scotland the remote and thinly-peopled parts of the country, " where but few duties accrue, are laid out in preventive districts, " instead of collections. A supervisor has charge of each of these " preventive districts, and acts in the capacity both of a check " officer and a receiver of duties. He has under him, in addition to " the ordinary surveying officers, a number of preventive officers " and preventive men, whose special business it is to aid in sup- " pressing the illicit manufacture of malt and spirits.

" In Ireland, since the abolition of the revenue police force, the

" same object is effected by the co-operation of the constabulary
" with the officers of excise.

" According to the latest arrangement :—

	Collections.	Districts.	Preventive Districts.	Divisions.	Rides.
England, with Wales, is divided into .... }	64	281	—	905	762
Scotland	13	63	9	313	85
Ireland	14	53	—	144	172
Total	91	397	9	1,362	1,019

—" Report of Commissioners of Inland Revenue, 1870," p. 5.

" In connection with this subject, that is, the additions which
" may be made to the revenue by a closer and more careful assess-
" ment and collection of existing duties, we cannot refrain from
" repeating an often expressed conviction, that the assessed taxes, if
" entirely taken out of the hands of parochial officers and entrusted
" to the sole management of this department, may be made to yield
" a much larger quota to the income of the country than at present.
" And we believe, that since we first began to ventilate the subject,
" a great change has taken place in public opinion respecting the
" antiquated, cumbrous, and inefficient system absurdly named ' self
" ' taxation,' and that there will be no difficulty now in superseding
" it by a better arrangement."*

" The financial year in which we are writing will be memorable
" in the history of this department. The reform we have so long
" advocated in the mode of collecting the assessed taxes has at
" length been effected, and effected more thoroughly and more
" satisfactorily than we had ventured to expect.

" It will be in your Lordships' recollection that we have been
" for many years urging the abolition of the system of collection
" and assessment of a branch of our revenue, through persons un-
" connected with the Executive Government. We pointed out that
" they were for the most part utterly indifferent to the interests of
" the Exchequer; that they had even been sometimes openly opposed
" to those interests, and engaged in doing their best to thwart the

* The following conversation, which really occurred between a member of this
department and a parochial assessor is worth preserving as an illustration :—
" A.—I see that Mr. B is not in assessment for either a horse or a carriage,
" though you know he keeps both.
" ASSESSOR (who is the principal butcher in the village).—Well, Sir, you must
" not be hard on a poor man like me. Mr. B is my best customer; and if I were
" to charge him, after so many years that he has gone on without paying any tax,
" he would give all his custom to X at once."—" Twelfth Report of Commissioners of
" Inland Revenue, 1869," p. 29.

" intentions of the legislature; that they were, many of them,
" illiterate, many corrupt; that for the purpose of instructing
" them in their duties, and restraining them from doing wrong,
" both to the crown and the subject, it was necessary for the Govern-
" ment to maintain another large staff of officers to go over the same
" ground, and that after all precaution and expense there remained
" an amount of evasion of taxes which could scarcely be accounted
" for by mere carelessness or ignorance.

" It is almost invariably the practice to appoint the same persons
" to be assessors and collectors for assessed taxes as for land tax,
" and very generally for income tax also. There is no inconvenience,
" but rather an advantage in this, but the same cannot be said of
" the practice which widely prevails of conferring the offices of
" assessor and collector on the same individual. It arose from the
" fact that assessors of land and assessed taxes are unpaid, and
" having the opportunity of returning themselves to be the col-
" lectors, they secure the poundage which is attached to that office.
" This practice has extended to the income tax, with regard to
" which it is even more objectionable than in the case of the land
" and assessed taxes, while it is also without excuse, as assessors of
" income tax are entitled to the same poundage as the collectors,
" viz., three half-pence in the pound on the amount of duties paid
" over by the collectors to the revenue. Great facility for fraud is
" thus afforded, and cases have occurred where collectors have
" received and appropriated to their own use large sums paid in
" discharge of returns which had been rendered to them in their
" capacity of assessors, instead of to the clerks to the Commis-
" sioners. The returns they had either suppressed or destroyed,
" and thus no charge was raised against them for the duty."—
" Report of the Commissioners of Inland Revenue, 1870," p. 103.

No systematic arrangement like that of the Inland Revenue
Commissioners is found in the administration of the local taxation
of the country generally. It exists certainly in one portion of the
organisation of one department—that of the Poor Law Board. In
their Twenty-second Annual Report, 1869-70, the audit districts
under their control are referred to.* In the Return 16, 1866,
"Local Government," referring to audits, many details may be found
respecting the local audits, which tend to show how incomplete they
are. Several remarks occur to the same effect in the evidence before
the Select Committee. "In the year 1864 the Select Committee
" of the House of Commons on Poor Relief recommended that the

---

* In the Return 16, 1866, "Local Government," referring to audits, many
details may be found respecting the local audits which tend to show how incomplete they are. Several remarks occur to the same effect in the evidence before
the Select Committee.

" number of the then existing audit districts should be reduced as
" vacancies occurred, and the vacant districts incorporated with
" others, the object of the recommendation being to make the audit
" districts sufficiently large to render it necessary that the auditors
" should devote the whole of their time to the public service. Since
" that period we have given effect, as far as practicable, to the
" policy thus indicated. There are still a large number of districts
" which require to be dissolved and amalgamated with others, and it
" is our intention to deal with them in this manner as far as prac-
" ticable, when vacancies occur."—" Report, 1869-70," p. 64.

The Poor Law audit deserves attention as being of an efficient
description, but it may be observed that it refers in some respects
more to the expenditure than to the levy of the rates, and that it
in no way applies to a check on those openings for fraud which
may occur in the collection. Many of the local officers, beyond
doubt, perform their duties most efficiently; they attend carefully
to the interests of their localities, and are honest and upright. Still,
the story reported by the Commissioners of Inland Revenue* might
perhaps find a parallel elsewhere, and there is no doubt great
ignorance and great carelessness among some, especially in remote
country parishes, while it is very possible that the slackness of
supervision permits, to say the least, the possibility of peculation.

The want of publicity in the amount of assessment, as well as of
the percentage of each rate, gives some further opening for fraud.
Every taxpayer knows exactly the proportions and percentage of
the income tax, the licence duties, the stamp duties, are arranged
on a clear and intelligible system. The excise duties are probably
as well known to those *on* whom as to those *by* whom they are
levied. If a penny in the pound is added to the income tax the
whole country is aware of it. But does any analogous knowledge
of the subject exist with regard to local taxation. Does it often
occur to a ratepayer to make himself sure that the amount which
his house stands at for the purpose of rating in the overseers'
accounts, is the same as that stated in the rate collectors' books,
either of demand notes or receipts? A different scale of deduction from the rateable value exists for different rates. It would
require more knowledge than is usually possessed by the ordinary
ratepayer, to detect the imposition if he were charged for both
systems of rates on the same footing. If the ratepayer has ascertained the rateable value of his premises, and has made himself
certain that the deductions are made on the proper scale, does he
often also ascertain that the amount in the pound for which he is
charged corresponds with the rate made? Does not the demand

* *Vide* note, p. 32, and also for the opinion of the Inland Revenue Department, on the local assessors and collectors, p. 33.

note frequently inform him for the first time of the amount of the rate? If the collector continued a higher rate, or mis-stated the figures to his own advantage, how many ratepayers, even of an educated sort, would have discovered the fraud? In giving this hint, it will be understood that no charge is meant to be brought against a body of men, as such, who in many cases discharge their duties honestly and efficiently, but it must at least be very obvious that great opportunities for fraud exist; and it is no less certain that such opportunities are liable to become very injurious to those who possess them.

VI.—*Consolidation of Local Rates.*

The consolidation of all local rates for all local purposes whatever; and the levying this consolidated rate at one, or at most at two periods of the year, would have many and great advantages over the existing system. The different local governing bodies should communicate their requirements to the proper authorities, who, on learning the amounts required, would proceed to levy the needful tax.

Since this was written Mr. Goschen has introduced a Bill for local rating and government, and has proposed that a consolidated rate, similar in great measure to that suggested above, should be made, and should be levied annually. On the demand note all the items for which the rate is levied will be stated, but the whole amount will be collected in one sum. Out of the fund thus raised all local authorities, town councils, local boards, boards of guardians, and others, will receive what they need. A complete provision for the collection of this consolidated rate and for the auditing of the expenditure is included. This plan promises to be a very great improvement on that hitherto in use. It will have the great advantage of keeping the control of the total expenditure of a parish under the supervision of one authority, instead of the subdivision now existing; a subdivision which tends to cause all sense of responsibility to be lost.

The plan of consolidating taxes, and collecting them at one time, has been found to work satisfactorily where it has been put into force. By Mr. Lowe's recent alteration in the method of collecting the income tax and the licence rates, which take the place of what used to be termed the assessed taxes, a very considerable sum is claimed from every taxpayer at the commencement of each year. Some objections were made to this at the time; objections which were best stated in an article in the " Economist," of 25th December, 1869; and mainly amounted to a doubt whether under existing arrangements an undesirable inequality was not caused in the amounts taken from the taxpayer at different times.

To consolidate all local charge into one rate, and to collect that rate annually, six months after the Government direct taxes are collected, would meet these objections to a great extent by counterbalancing the new year's claim of the Imperial Government with a midsummer claim of the parish, municipality, or county. The tax would be leviable by anticipation for the coming year, as the licences which take the place of the assessed taxes are now; this would extremely diminish the number of defaulters, and render fraud, for the broken period between the determination of one tenancy and the commencement of another, impossible.

An arrangement like this would go far to counterbalance the inequality complained of. The only point that might appear at first sight an objection is, that the amount thus proposed to be raised exceeds the totals of the duties levied at present in the January of each year. But there would be immediate advantages which would go far to compensate this, and other objections. It is almost certain, judging by experience in such matters, that great saving of expense would arise from the complete supervision of accounts; the more careful auditing; the greater exactness in every way which would be obtained. Nor must other points be overlooked. At present the vast sums raised for local purposes escape general attention from the manner in which they are levied. Few are aware till their attention is specially called to it, that the expenditure for the relief of the poor alone, is in many years a far heavier impost than the income tax, while the total levy for all local purposes is now far heavier than the highest income tax raised in this country since its re-imposition by Sir R. Peel, equivalent at this time to an income tax of 1s. 6d. in the pound.* If the total amount raised for local purposes were stated in one comprehensive report, with separate subsidiary reports for each locality, it would become an easy matter to compare the rating and outlay in different places. At present very little general knowledge on the subject exists. The variation between the rates of places close or contiguous to each other is generally known through the fact that individuals hold or occupy property in the different localities, or through the ordinary conversation of common life. But it is more than probable that the ratepayers, say of York, are entirely ignorant of the amounts levied in Ripon, except so far as some casual and imperfect intimation may reach them through a paragraph in the newspaper. And yet infor-

---

* Expenditure for the relief of the poor, 1867-68, 7,498,061l. "Report of "Poor Law Board, 1869-70," p. vii.

Income tax, year ended 31st March, 1868, 6,184,166l. Rate 4d. in the pound. —"Report of Commissioners of Inland Revenue," p. 3.

Estimate of total amount raised by local taxation in the United Kingdom for 1870, 25,000,000l.—"Statistical Abstract, 1870," p. 5.

mation on such points is eminently desirable; there may be, perhaps, some better form of administration in the one place as compared with the other, which might be a very useful thing to be known.

The only means of conveying this information at present existing, beyond those mentioned above, which are manifestly inadequate, are found in the Annual Reports of the Poor Law Board, and in the recently published Returns on Local Taxation. The reports just named are of the greatest service in their several ways, but they only include portions of the subject. An annual return including a general and comprehensive report, with an appendix divided into pamphlets of a convenient size, in the same manner as the volumes of the Irish Census, would give the means of diffusing authentic intelligence throughout the kingdom.

The local rate thus levied would continue to be administered by the municipal authorities in all cities and boroughs. The consolidation of the payments would afford in most instances continuous occupation for the collectors, who should devote the whole of their time to the business. If the local levy were small, the authorities might advantageously avail themselves of the assistance of the officers of the Inland Revenue. In rural parishes the requisite notices might easily be distributed through the post offices, where the local rates might likewise be paid. One principle for assessment should prevail, with a uniform system of deductions.

It would greatly simplify matters if every tenement or property rated to local rates were numbered, and had this number marked on it in some suitable manner. This number would equally apply to the occupier, whether owner or tenant. It should correspond with the number in the rate-book, and in the register for voting, whether parochial or municipal, county or parliamentary. This number would be marked on the demand note or assessment paper, which would be annually left at each dwelling; and by it the tax payer would be readily recognised when he went to the tax office of his district. The production of the receipt would identify the tax payer at the polling place when he went to vote at a parochial, municipal, county, or parliamentary election. The case of the " compound householder" would for this purpose present no difficulty. His habitation would likewise receive its number, and it should be made compulsory on the landlord, within a reasonable time after the delivery of the receipt to him, to deliver the same to the occupier. To prevent personation, it would be needful to limit the right of voting to those electors who had gone themselves to the guildhall of the local government, and signed their names on the register, and at the back of the receipt at the same time. If it be objected, how would this meet the cases of those unable from want of education to sign their own names, it may be replied, can those who are unable to meet this lowest test of education be fit to exercise the franchise ? A limitation as to the time before this provision should be brought into effect would obviate much difficulty, and arrangements could easily be made for keeping the offices of the local governments open at such hours as would be suitable for all classes.

It might be possible to save much of the expense of collection, by charging a percentage on all rates not brought to the local office within a certain stipulated date, after the time when the rate was made. This percentage would defray some of the cost of collection, while the bringing the remainder to the local office by the ratepayers themselves would, by rendering fewer local officers necessary, tend to diminish expense. The rate being levied annually, at a fixed date, would greatly facilitate these arrangements.

Nor would such a method in any way interfere with existing arrangements. Those rates which are now levied locally would continue to be so levied, only with the great advantage of a trained staff of officers and a careful system.

Another desideratum would be more easily attained than under the existing mode of collection, viz., the consolidation of the local administration. As matters stand at present, there can hardly be fewer than two, there are generally more, governing bodies in every locality. The guardians of the poor administer their portion ; the board of health do their share ; the town councils, the county magistrates, to mention only some of the most prominent governing bodies, have their own functions as well. The school boards already appointed in many places, likely soon to be very general, if not universal, will, like those governing bodies previously named, have their own power of rating, with, it is to be presumed, all the authority of the other boards. The Sanitary Commissioners of 1870, looking at the subject from another point of view, have arrived at the same opinion.

" We now wish to lay the utmost stress upon the importance
" of taking every possible step towards introducing coincidence
" between the areas of petty sessions, highway districts, and unions
" which will be rural districts.

" Unions, and sometimes even parishes, overlapping county boun-
" daries ; registration districts making incomplete correspondence
" with them in statistics of births and deaths ; highway districts
" made optionally, and irrespectively of all other areas, or coinciding
" sometimes with one, sometimes with another ; petty sessional
" divisions generally differing from all ; cause altogether to a
" country whose life is self-administration, probably the maximum
" of embarrassment and waste of local government, and the utmost
" loss of means and effectiveness.

" The same boundaries should, as far as possible, define the
" areas of all these kinds of provincial executive, and their officers,
" should be, as far as possible, the same for all those purposes."—
" Report of the Sanitary Commission, 1870," p. 53.

It is scarcely within the scope of this work to go more into
detail upon the composition of such a general board for local
finance as is here suggested. It cannot be doubted but that great
confusion in the fiscal system would take place, and in all probability.
vast needless expenditure be incurred, if one amount of tax were
levied to maintain the army, another to provide for the navy, a
third to defray the expenses of the civil list ; and if all these different
taxes were charged on nearly the same property, but with differing
classifications, and raised and administered by different boards, acting
independently of each other. Yet this is but a faint picture of the
existing local administration in England. Mr. Goschen's words on
the 3rd April, 1871, on bringing in the Government measures for
regulating local taxation, and for local government, describe the
present state of matters very forcibly :—" The truth is, that we have
" a chaos as regards authorities, a chaos as regards rates, and a worse
" chaos than all as regards areas. And not only that, but every
" different form of collection which it is possible to conceive is applied
" to the various local authorities administering these various rates in
" these various areas." The proposed parochial boards and county
financial boards will, it is to be hoped, provide the remedy recommended above. It is now desirable to proceed to a consideration of
the system employed in Scotland and Ireland.

VII.—Scotland.

In Scotland, the principle of dividing great part of the local
taxation between the owner and the occupier of land appears to
have prevailed from time immemorial. This principle is contained
in the old Scotch statutes, which are the foundation of the Scotch
poor laws ; those statutes contemplated that half of the entire sum
should come from the land and the other half from the inhabitants.*
The existing Scotch Poor Law Act was passed in 1845, by which
parochial boards were empowered to raise the necessary funds for
the relief of the poor, in three different ways :—

I. By resolving that half the rate be imposed on the owners,
and half on the occupiers of all lands and heritages.

II. By assessing half on the owners, according to the value of
their lands, and half on the whole of the inhabitants, according to
their means and substance other than lands and tenements.

* " Report of the Select Committee on Local Taxation." Evidence of *Mr. F.
J. Cochran*, 354.

III. By assessment, as an equal percentage upon the annual value of all lands and heritages, and upon the estimated annual income of the whole of the inhabitants from means and substance other than land heritages.*

Practically speaking, the poor law assessment now is always raised according to the first method. "The system in Scotland was "to rate the owner uniformly till within recent years, when the "present poor law was passed. The occupier then had to pay half "the rates for the first time. That, however, was not altogether a "new payment, though it was a payment in a different manner, "because formerly, before there was any poor law, the paupers "were allowed to beg in the country. They had the privilege of "begging, and were supplied in kind by the farmers, and that pay- "ment in kind was, to great extent, converted into money under "the new poor law."†

Macclesfield was given as an example of English municipal government; in a similar way we may take Aberdeen, described in the evidence of Mr. J. Cochran, as an instance for Scotland. Mr. Cochran, besides being much employed in the assessment and collection of the county rates, poor rates, income tax, &c., has, with his firm, charge of very considerable heritable property, both in the city and county.

In Scotland, nearly as great a diversity of rates appears to exist as in England, and a greater diversity even in the assessment; but in the governing bodies, in the mode of assessment, especially as regards the poor rate, and in the way in which the collection is administered, the advantage rests with those dwelling north of the Tweed.

The rates for the county of Aberdeen consist of the following, besides the poor's rates assessed as just mentioned :—

The County General Assessment.
The Police Assessment.
The Prisons Assessment.
The Militia Depôt Assessment.
The Registration of Voters Assessment.
The Aberdeen County and Municipal Buildings Assessment.
The Cattle Diseases Prevention Assessment.
The Turnpike Road Assessment.
The Commutation Road Debt Assessment.
The Roads Maintenance or Repair Assessment.
The Roads Construction Assessment.

---

* "Report of the Select Committee on Local Taxation." Evidence of Mr. J. Lambert, 2339.
† Ibid. Evidence of Mr. J. Caird, 4131.

Of these, the commutation road debt assessment is parochial, and only applies when a commutation road debt is in existence. The road repair assessment is over the whole county, but varies within each of the districts for which the county is divided for that purpose. The four different road assessments are in virtue of a local Act. All these various rates are raised from the owner only. But the arrangement as to the road maintenance rate, and the cattle diseases rate is, that the landlord may recover half the tax from the tenant. In all the other cases the tax falls entirely on the landlord.

With regard to the borough rates.—In the city of Aberdeen, besides the poor rates, there are the police assessment, which includes watching, lighting, water, and certain criminal expenditure; a public health rate and a municipal building rate, under the charge of the commissioners of police; and the rogue money, spent in paying the procurator fiscal, or public prosecutor, and in the apprehending of criminals and the detection of crime. All these are levied on the occupier.

The prisons assessment, the valuation assessment, the registration of births and of voters assessment, under the charge of the lord provost and magistrates. The militia depôt, the roads assessment (under borough road trustees), are levied equally on the owner and occupier.

The sewer rate under the charge of the police commissioners, the county and municipal buildings and court house assessments (under the charge of the lord provost and magistrates), are on the owner only.

Whatever proportions of these rates are paid by the owner and occupier are collected separately from the owner and occupier; the doing this involves "additional labour," "and a great many more " entries in the books."*

To illustrate the mode of assessment in a Scotch parish, half rural half urban, it is as well to cite the plan which Mr. Cochran set going in Old Machar, a parish containing nearly half the city of Aberdeen and five or six miles of farms outside it. Here, in order to avoid levying different rates on the inhabitants who were liable in different proportions, an arrangement was made to charge a uniform rate, but on different proportions of the rent.

The plan was as follows :—

" Rules of assessment for the poor of the parish of Old Machar, " under the Act 8 and 9 Vict., cap. 83, intituled 'An Act for the " ' Amendment and better Administration of the Laws relating

* *Vide* evidence of *Mr. F. J. Cochran, Mr. Lambert,* and *Mr. Caird,* before Select Committee of the House of Commons, 1870.

" ' to the Relief of the Poor in Scotland.' One-half of the whole
" assessment required for the parish shall be imposed upon the
" owners and the other half upon the tenants or occupants of all
" lands and heritages within the parish, rateably according to the
" annual value of such lands and heritages, and in levying each half
" the following rules shall be observed. As to classification of lands :
" the lands and heritages in the parish of Old Machar shall, for the
" purposes of the assessment on the tenants or occupants, be distin-
" guished into three separate classes; the first class consisting
" of dwelling-houses and whole other lands and heritages, except
" those mentioned in the second and third classes ; the second consist-
" ing of shops, warehouses, and stables used solely in the occupier's
" trade or business, business offices, spinning mills, manufactories,
" brick works, quarries, water powers and railways, gas pipes,
" water pipes, and ground used for such pipes ; and the third class
" consisting of farms, cultivated grounds, and fishings ; and that
" the rates of assessment upon the tenants or occupants as such
" shall be so fixed as that the rate upon those of the second of
" the said classes shall be as nearly as possible one-half, and the
" rate upon those of the third class as nearly as possible one-fourth
" part respectively of the rate upon those of the first class."*

The outcome of the scheme was that the—

	s.	d.	
Owners were rated at	–	9	in the pound
Occupiers, Class 1	1	1½	„
„ 2	–	7	„
„ 3	–	3½	„

the owners paying 4,275*l.*, the occupiers 4,733*l.*, " or (deducting
" arrears, &c.) as near as might be one-half of the whole."

The local government of Aberdeen itself, with the number of
different authorities mentioned above, appears to be nearly, if not
quite, as complicated as that of Macclesfield. In the parish of
Old Machar the poor law administration is conducted by a board of
supervision. This does not meet above thrice in the year, and has
full power to delegate their entire functions to various committees
for the conduct of special portions of the business. The board
consists of four different constituent bodies—owners of lands and
heritages of the value of 20*l.* and upwards, and any agent appointed
in writing by a heritor entitled to be a member of the board; the
provost and baillies of the borough; the kirk session, consisting of
the minister and elders, who, if numbering more than six, have
to send only six from their number; and the elected members, about
twenty in number. As there are about 1,500 20*l.* proprietors in

* *Mr. F. J. Cochran's* evidence to the Select Committee of the House of
Commons, p. 18 (325).

the parish, little interest is taken in the choice of elected members, who form but a fractional part of the entire board. The whole arrangement seems to be a cumbrous one, but in Mr. Cochran's opinion it has worked pretty well.

Purely urban parish boards are constituted on a different system. In St. Nicholas, Aberdeen, for instance, fifteen members are elected by the ratepayers, four by the magistrates of the borough, four more by the kirk session. In rural parishes the boards are constituted as in the instance given above of Old Machar; except, of course, as to the provost and baillies where no royal burgh is situated in the parish.

The county rates are raised by commissioners of supply, who are " all the proprietors who own a life rent in lands, or who have " a life rent in lands of the yearly value of 100l., or who are " owners in fee to that value, also the eldest son and the heir " apparent of the proprietor in fee of rents to the amount of 400l., " and the factor of any proprietor in fee in the absence of the " proprietor who possesses lands of the yearly value of 800l."— " Report of Local Taxation, 1870," *Mr. J. Lambert.*

" There are no local taxation returns from Scotland which " bring together the total expenditure, such as exist in England and " Ireland." See Mr. Goschen's question 2356, in " Report of the " Select Committee on Local Taxation, 1870."

The absence of this information prevents the possibility of an exact comparison between Scotland and England, but it may be said that the Scotch method of giving those permanently interested in the fixed property of a place, whether in houses or land, in conjunction with the occupiers, so great a power over the local taxation, appears to have acted in a very beneficial manner for the interests of the inhabitants of that part of Great Britain. The reasons for this are well summed up in the following observations made by Mr. Caird :—

" In Scotland we have found that the owner, from being " directly called upon to pay a large proportion of the rates, takes " a very active interest in their administration, and I think that has " led to much economy, and also probably to a more liberal and far " seeing view of the position of affairs in the district, than would " be the case when it falls entirely upon the occupying tenant."

Mr. Caird added—

" I think there is a great advantage in getting the occupier to " feel an interest as far as the management of the labouring poor " and of roads are concerned, because there are many cases in which " he has a very direct interest, and a great deal of knowledge of " the matter. I think it is of very great advantage to get this " personal interest in the administration of those matters."— *Mr. J. Caird's* " Evidence to the Select Committee, 1870," p. 196.

An abstract of the poor law expenditure in Scotland during the years 1846-68 inclusive is given in Table R. The difficulty in comparing even this portion of the local taxation with that of the rest of Great Britain, is enhanced by the manner in which the ratio in the pound of the poor's rate to the rateable value is computed. The returns of 1843 are taken as a basis, and the differences resulting are thus explained:—

"Although it has been thought desirable, for the purpose of "comparison with former years, to show in the preceding table the "rate per cent. on the annual value of real property as returned in "1843, it is right to state that, according to the annual value "returned in 1856, the rate per cent. for the last twelve years would "be as follows:—

	£	s.	d.		£	s.	d.
Year ended 14th May, 1856	5	7	6¾	Year ended 14th May, 1863	6	5	9½
" '57	5	8	9	" '64	6	11	7¼
" '58	5	9	6¼	" '65	6	13	–¼
" '59	5	12	4¼	" '66	6	13	10¼
" '60	5	13	4¼	" '67	6	18	–½
" '61	5	16	10¾	" '68	7	7	6½
" '62	6	3	–¼				

"The rate per cent. for 1868 on the annual value of real property, "as estimated for 1859, would be *6l.* 13*s.* 11½*d.*, or 1*l.* 6*s.* 4¾*d.* per "cent. greater than in 1856 when similar returns were available."— "Twenty-third Annual Report of Poor Law Board for Scotland," p. xiv.

It would appear, according to this statement, that the rate of the poor law expenditure in Scotland was 5*s.* 7½*d.* per head of the population in 1869, as compared with 7*s.* –¾*d.* per head in England, and the local taxation generally seems to press less severely on the available revenues of the former than of the latter country.

VIII.—*Ireland.*

Ireland differs as to system of local taxation both from England and Scotland. The principle of the representation of the taxpayer appears more completely attained in Ireland than in England, but there is an absence of the prominence given to the landowner in Scotland. The general system is thus described by Dr. Hancock:—

"The grand jury cess is a tax peculiar to Ireland. The pur"poses for which it is raised are chiefly those provided in England "and Wales by the highway rate, turnpike tolls, county rates, rates "for bridges, and police rate. As to its incidence it may be divided "into two parts—one for general objects, levied off the entire of each "county or county of a city or a town; and the other for objects of a

" more local character, levied of each barony or half barony of a
" county, a division of the country which corresponds to a hundred
" in England. The cess is levied by an equal poundage rate on
" the occupiers of landed property in each barony or half barony.
" The kind of property liable to assessment corresponds very
" closely to that rateable to the poor rate in England and
" Wales.

" The origin of the jurisdiction of grand juries in Ireland over
" roads and bridges dates so far back as the reign of King Charles I,
" when by statute 10 Car. I, cap. 26, sec. 2 (Irish), correspond-
" ing to 22 Henry VIII, cap. 5 (English), the justices of assize and
" of the peace were directed to inquire what bridges in the county
" were broken down or out of repair, and to award process on
" presentment against such persons as were chargeable with the
" repair. If the persons liable were unknown, the expense was to
" be borne by the inhabitants of the county or barony where the
" bridge was situate, and the justices were directed to tax the
" inhabitants 'reasonably' for that purpose, with the assent of the
" grand jury. This appears to have been intended as a statutable
" substitute for the common law remedy and procedure by indict-
" ment, which, of course, would be of no avail where the parties
" liable could not be ascertained. The sanction of the grand jury
" to the taxation of the justices is quite peculiar to Ireland ; the
" corresponding Act of Henry VIII required the assent of the
" constables, or the inhabitants of the city, town, or parish.

" From this commencement a whole code of local legislation
" peculiar to Ireland has arisen. In 1836 the power of the grand
" juries was limited by the creation of a tribunal called presentment
" sessions for each barony and for the county at large, consisting of
" the magistrates of the county and a certain number of the highest
" cesspayers chosen by ballot out of a list fixed by the grand jury.
" Nearly all the presentments as to which the grand jury have any
" discretion are required to be first passed at these presentment
" sessions.

" The constitution of these presentment sessions has been lately
" fully considered by the Select Committee of the House of Com-
" mons upon grand jury presentments, which sat during the session
" of 1868, and propositions recommending the entire abolition of
" both sessions and grand jury, and the substitution of elective
" baronial and county boards, were fully discussed. The Com-
" mittee, however, recommend that the present bodies should be
" retained, but with some modifications, which, if adopted, will
" have the effect of making the sessions more representative of the
" general body of the cesspayers."—" Returns of Local Taxation in
" Ireland, 1869," p. 5.

Local Taxation in Ireland, as Compared with that in England.

" As stated in my former report" (Dr. Hancock observes, in
1869), " the valuations in the two countries admit of only a very
" general comparison, as they are made under very different autho-
" rities. The Irish valuation undergoes an annual revision in detail,
" so far as the changes of occupation, or as the deterioration or
" improvement in the value of buildings is concerned, but this does
" not affect the gross value of each townland, exclusive of buildings,
" which remains a constant sum from year to year, capable of
" alteration only at the end of each period of fourteen years, and
" even then only upon the application of the grand jury of the
" county. In the northern counties, where the valuation has been
" comparatively recent, it is believed to be within 20 per cent.
" of the fair letting value of land on good estates, not including the
" interest of yearly tenants or buildings; while in the south, where
" no alteration has been made in the basis adopted in the valuation
" made during the period following the famine of 1846-47, when
" the poor rates were high, and the state of agriculture depressed,
" the valuation is believed to be still more below the letting value.
" To whatever extent this is the case, the poundage rate of local
" taxation in Ireland appears higher than it really is.

" If the amount of local taxation (including all sums of receipts
" except money borrowed) in the two countries, be compared in
" proportion to the population, the following results appear:—

	£
Estimated local taxation of Ireland, 1868	2,804,717
„ England and Wales	20,145,884
Amount of local taxation on a portion of the population of England and Wales equal to the population of Ireland	5,825,927
Amount by which the local taxation of Ireland is less than the local taxation on an equal portion of the population of England and Wales.............................	3,021,210

" It appears from the above that the local taxation of Ireland is
" 3,021,210*l.* less than it would be if the scale of local taxation per
" head of the population was the same as in England and Wales.

" It appears also that the rate of local taxation levied in
" Ireland in 1868, may be estimated at 9*s.* 2*d.* per head, whilst the
" rate of local taxation in England and Wales in the same year may
" be estimated at 1*l.* –*s.* 3*d.* per head."—" Returns of Local Taxa-
" tion in Ireland, 1869."

To arrive, however, at an estimate of the expenditure corresponding to the total local taxation of England, the charge for the
Irish Constabulary Force, defrayed from the consolidated fund,
should be added to this sum; the amount of the vote for the current
year, 1871, was 843,007*l.*

A discrepancy in the returns is pointed out in the " Report of
" the Irish Poor Law Commissioners for 1869."

" It will be seen that the total disbursement of poor rates for
" all purposes, viz., relief, medical relief, burial grounds, registration
" of births, deaths, and marriages, and sanitary measures, was in
" 1868, 847,995*l.*, and the amount of poor rate collected 848,070*l.*,
" the levy and expenditure each making a poundage of 1*s.* 3$\frac{1}{2}$*d.* in
" the pound on the valuation. In 1869 the expenditure fell to
" 817,772*l.*, or 1*s.* 2$\frac{3}{4}$*d.* in the pound, and the poor rate collected to
" 815,480*l.*

" In a volume entitled 'Local Taxation, Ireland,' which has
" been laid by Her Majesty's command before Parliament, that part
" of the Irish local taxation for 1868 which consists of poor rate,
" is incorrectly stated to have been 921,807*l.*,* and the poundage
" thereof to be 1*s.* 5*d.* in the pound on the valuation. This overstate-
" ment arises from the parliamentary grant having been included
" as part of that year's taxation. The grant, however, is provided
" from the imperial funds, and is no part of the local taxation of
" Ireland. Neither does it represent in any way the local expendi-
" ture of that year; for the grant is practically a recoup of
" the expenditure in the previous year. In fact, for many years
" past, neither the levy of poor rates nor the expenditure has
" exceeded 1*s.* 3$\frac{1}{2}$*d.* in the pound, and has usually been much below
" it."—" Annual Report of the Commissioners for Administering
" the Laws for Relief of the Poor in Ireland, 1870," p. 20.

IX.—*Some Other Points in Local Taxation.*

Some incidental but important points were reserved for further
consideration in the outline of the main question given above.
Among these are the objections which have been made to the
manner in which the existing local taxation is raised, and to defraying certain charges from local funds.

These have been put by Sir M. Lopes, with regard to the
assessment on land employed for agricultural purposes, in a very
forcible manner. Sir M. Lopes stated that "a man purchasing
" a large estate, with the buildings dilapidated and the land
" undrained, invested a considerable sum in the necessary improve-
" ments, and was immediately assessed on those improvements.
" Why should he pay local taxation on the money thus invested
" more than if it had remained perhaps in the foreign funds ? So,
" again, a man rented a farm for fourteen years. He found that
" unless he spent a large sum in manure it would be a ruinous

---

* The total local taxation for the year 1869, is given in Table S. No further
analysis is attempted, the absence of a police rate, in general, for Ireland, affecting
the totals so much as to prevent any useful comparison with England.

" undertaking.   He borrowed money for the purpose, and imme-
" diately the assessment committee came down upon him and made
" him pay local taxation on the personal property he had borrowed
" and invested in it."*

The answer to objections of this class is twofold :—That those
who acted thus thought it worth while to do so ;

That so far as the grievance exists, it is not an agricultural
grievance only.

The purchaser of the let-down estate in the one case, the hirer
in the other, undoubtedly considered that they obtained, in consequence of the land being so much " run out," a cheaper bargain
in proportion to condition than they could have done elsewhere,
otherwise they would not have bought or hired it.   It is true that
some experienced land agents hold the contrary opinion ; namely,
that land, when let down in condition, never sinks as low in value
as is proportionate to that condition ; but there are, doubtless,
exceptional cases.   At all events, these persons thought otherwise.
They thought it worth while to enter on these bargains ; they
considered, perhaps truly, that the money invested in improvements
was not only well secured, but would yield a larger return when so
employed than it did before.   Large enough, in the one instance, to
reproduce the dividends presumably obtainable from the "foreign
" funds ;" in the other, to provide the interest on the capital
borrowed after paying all outgoings, in which the usual local
taxation bore a share.   Nor is the hardship these persons complained of confined to the improvements of agricultural land only.
Had the landowner or the farmer instanced, employed their capital
in effecting similar improvements upon dilapidated house property
in any town, they would have found the local assessors there equally
alive to any marked rise in the value of a manufactory, an office,
or a shop.

The practical consideration arising is, that the amount of local
taxation should not be, as now, a local matter only ; but that it
should be considered in its relation to imperial taxation as well.
A particular and unlooked-for pressure of local taxation on one
form of investment alone, such as an investment in agricultural
improvements, would be a peculiarly objectionable impost.   If the
burden of taxation of any improvement of what is technically
termed real property, whether that consists of lands or tenements,
becomes, or is, so onerous as to amount to a real bar to' the
improvement of that description of property, it is the duty of the
Government to inquire into the matter, and to adjust the local
taxation in such a manner as to prevent this from occurring.

* From report of speech made by Sir M. Lopes, in the debate on local
taxation, House of Commons, 21st February, 1870.

Otherwise the general prosperity of the country, so far as it depends on such improvements, will receive a check which may be prejudicial to it in the highest degree. It would be an evil day for the country should the small capitalist—the owner of, say from 3,000*l.* to 5,000*l.*—find that it answered his purpose better to keep his money in some foreign stock and content himself with drawing the dividends as they became due, and living on the proceeds, instead of investing the capital in some occupation which would offer the ordinary profits of trade, being deterred by the pressure of local taxation on the industrial occupations of the country.

The abolition of exemptions of Government property would, in the existing state of matters, be clearly an act of justice. Every trade, every manufacture, has a tendency to attract labour to its vicinity, and, with the present habits of our working population, an increase of the poor rates is almost certain to follow such an aggregation of working men. Sanitary measures become also requisite, and considerable expense is thus entailed. There can be no equitable reason why a Government factory or dockyard should not be charged with local rates exactly in the same manner as a private concern of a similar nature. The same principle applies in some other cases. Some descriptions of property are only partially rateable, or assessed on so different a principle as amount to a practical exemption.* Thus, though "saleable underwoods" are rateable, plantations made for ornament or for shelter to game are only so when there is underwood which is felled periodically. Plantations are, however, rateable for the herbage growing between the trees, generally at about 1*s.* per acre. Parks are rated according to the rent they will command, which may differ very much from the agricultural or other value. As an extreme case, Holland House and Park may be cited. The gross assessment is 1,400*l.*; and net, according to the ratio used for all in Kensington parish, 1,167*l.* This is for the house and park. About half the assessment may be put on the park of 150 acres. The remarks on Lord Sefton's unused land at Liverpool, No. 2956, Evidence Select Committee, Mr. H. C. Beloe, are curious. The right of shooting appears to be rateable if let separately from the land;† but not rateable if retained in the owner's possession.‡ Such alterations would, however, only affect a few places. The same is to be said as to the assessment of mines. This would add only about six millions and a-half to the present rateable value of about 100 millions. But though these alterations would be only local in their influence, and no general

---

* The details of the properties expressly liable are given in Appendix, No. I.
† *Vide* Meyrick *v.* Battle Union, "Justice of the Peace," 30, p. 727.
‡ *Vide* Reg. *v.* Thurstone, 1 E. and E., 502; but Chief Justice Cockburn throws a doubt upon that decision in Meyrick *v.* Battle Union.

E

effect can be looked for from such measures, it is desirable that such exemptions should cease.

On the other hand, the owners of some descriptions of property, for instance tithes, complain that their property is over assessed in proportion to other property. The amount of the rent charge in each parish is accurately known, and on this amount the clergyman or titheholder is assessed. The assessment of the rest of the parish is generally made by farmers, the persons most concerned in keeping their own ratings low, and the amount of their payments to their landlords may not be a matter of equal notoriety with the tithe. The principles on which deductions are made from the gross value assessed appear to differ materially in the cases of the farmer and the parson, be he vicar or rector. For instance, until recently, a deduction was allowed from the total value of the living, in cases where the exigencies of population and area obviously made the employment of a curate in addition to the incumbent a necessity. This exemption has been recently annulled by a decision in the Court of Queen's Bench.* No deduction either is allowed for payments made by the incumbent to the "Queen Anne's Bounty Fund" in the cases where a living is mortgaged to the governors of that fund for the repairs or rebuilding of the parsonage house. These payments, however, certainly appear to come within the statutable deductions which are to be made from the gross, in order to arrive at the rateable value, among which deductions the cost of repairs is particularly specified. There appears to be ground for a belief that an inequality of assessment exists in these cases, and that attention should be called to them whenever existing arrangements are revised.

The incidence of local taxation on railways, gasworks, and waterworks appears extremely disproportionate to that on other industrial undertakings, which, while carrying on businesses on a large scale, have no "visible and local" connection with the land, except in regard to the houses or other premises which they may occupy. A bank, a discount company, or a brewery company, to take some familiar instances, may be carrying on their respective trades, employing large capitals, gaining large profits, but the percentage which they pay to local taxation will be far smaller in proportion than that which is imposed on railways, and the other similar industrial associations named above. In the case of a banking company, the rating is on the rental of the premises occupied, which rental probably is but a very small part of the expenses of carrying on the business. In the case of the railway, the gas-

* Reg. v. Sherford, " Justice of the Peace," 31, p. 436.

The inconveniences arising from legislating on one part of the subject of rating alone, are shown in Appendix II.

works, or the waterworks, as the company is not only the owner
but the occupier, a hypothetical tenancy is supposed to exist, and
the net value, for the purpose of rating, is arrived at by deducting
the expenses of working from the gross profit, and by then making
certain further allowances for the maintenance of those portions of
the materials employed (e.g., the permanent way of a railway)
which are most liable to deterioration. A hypothetical valuation of
a railway was given by Mr. Edward Ryde, in a paper read before
the Institution of Surveyors, 28th November, 1870, and is subjoined
here in a condensed form :—

	£
Gross receipts of railway (say)	500,000
Deduct working expenses, maintenance of way, &c.	250,000
	250,000
Deduct occupiers' share, interest on capital, &c.	125,000
	125,000
Statutable deductions, renewal of way, &c.	20,000
Rateable value	105,000

The result is, that the rating is based, to a great extent, on the
profits earned by the concern; while in the case of an ordinary
industrial company, profits do not enter into the account. In the
case of a farm, for instance, it is the rent, not the presumed profit
of the farmer, which forms the basis of the rateable value. The
legislature has, in some cases, recognised the principle that the
incidence of local taxation on these companies is unduly severe.
According to the Health of Towns Act, railways, canals, and
waterworks are only assessed at one-fourth of their ordinary rateable value for the rates levied under that Act. When canals were
first introduced into this country, the legislature, contemplating the
benefits which such undertakings would confer on the districts
through which they passed, and considering that the ordinary
methods of assessment did not apply to such concerns, sanctioned
arrangements according to which the canal was rated, in respect
of the land occupied, according to the value of the land adjacent,
a method which seems to afford a very fair basis.*

* "And be it further enacted, that the said company of proprietors of the said
" Worcester and Birmingham Canal shall, from time to time, be rated to all parlia-
" mentary and parochial taxes, rates, and assessments for, and in respect of the
" lands and hereditaments taken and used by the said company for the purposes of
" the said navigation; and all warehouses and other buildings erected, or to be
" erected thereon by the said company of proprietors by virtue of the said Act, and
" of this present Act, in the same proportions as other lands, grounds, and build-
" ings adjoining or lying near the said canal are, or shall be, rated."—Canal Rating
Clause, 38 Geo. III, cap. 31; see also 39 Geo. III, cap. 80, sec. 46, Stratford-upon-
Avon Canal.

In 1864, when a considerable clearance of house property, especially in the metropolis, was contemplated for railway extensions, it was provided that, as a great extent of rateable property would be destroyed, the railway company causing such a demolition should be rateable to the same amount as the property destroyed was rated at, until the railway was completed. No similar arrangement, it should be mentioned, has been made in any other case where property has been taken for purposes of improvement. The principle acted on was, that the parishes should not lose by the construction of the railway. The natural inference would appear to be, that the parishes should not ultimately gain. Under these circumstances, and with so many analogous points in their favour, it is not to be wondered at that the companies, thus exposed to a disproportionate taxation in respect of the rates levied on the poor rate series, have on every possible opportunity made every effort in their power to obtain a reduction. Every point has been contested. The amount of litigation attending on these assessments has been enormous, and in the vast majority of cases the assessment is arrived at by means of a compromise, and not by any certain and well considered method.

The late Mr. Justice Wightman, when delivering judgment in one case which came before him (that of the West Middlesex Waterworks Company), observed that the whole subject appeared to him to be involved in so much difficulty and uncertainty, that he could not but hope that the legislature might interfere or make some provision adapted to the rating of the property of such companies, which might declare the principle upon which such companies should be rated, and establish some uniform and practical mode of carrying that principle into effect. According to the method at present followed, the railway, the gas, or the water company is regarded as the occupier or owner of the extent of land improved by the industrial business carried on by the company. But if the basis adopted in rating canal property, as mentioned above, was not considered satisfactory, a fair method would appear to be to regard these companies as the owners of vast machines, either for the transport of passengers, or of water, or for the manufacture and distribution of gas. The viaducts, the tunnels of a railway, the mains of a water or a gas company, are certainly, strictly speaking, stock in trade to those concerns. The existing method of assessment according to the profits of the business they carry on, in respect of the land they occupy, is in fact to tax stock in trade, which in all other cases in England is exempt from local taxation. A very remarkable instance of the severity of this taxation is mentioned in the minutes of evidence taken before the Select Committee of the House of Commons on Valuations, &c., Land and

Assessments (Scotland) Bill, 1870. The instance referred to is that of a waterworks company, but it illustrates the method adopted with sufficient clearness.

The main conduit of the Glasgow Waterworks Company from Loch Katrine running towards Glasgow, commences in the parish of Aberfoil and opens into another parish. It thus passes entirely underground, completely through the parish of Aberfoil, entirely out of sight, causing neither injury to, nor disturbance of, the soil. As stated, " you may go through the parish and never know that " the thing is there." Yet the value of this tunnel or aqueduct and piping, as ascertained under the existing law for the purposes of rating, is 4,822*l.*, that is to say, the company is rated on the basis of 4,822*l.* to the parish for this "beneficial occupation." It is not to be wondered at that " the parishes and counties through which " the line of water pipes passed, were very agreeably surprised " when they understood the large value which was put upon these " works."* Gasworks and railways are proceeded with exactly in the same way. The method followed in Scotland by Mr. Dods, the appointed Assessor, in assessing railways and canals is as follows :—" I proceeded first to take the gross revenue of the " railway companies from all sources as a foundation, I then " deducted the working expenses, except the item for maintenance " of way. This brought out the net revenue.

" I then ascertained the value of the plant and rolling stock " employed by the companies in realising these profits, and allowed " 25 per cent. on that value, deducting which from the net revenue, " left the value to which the railway was subject for assessments. " This 25 per cent. embraced tenants' profits; some minor charges " were allowed for or apportioned."

The result in the case of the Glasgow and South Western Railway is as follows :—

Year Ending Whit-Sunday, 1870.

	£
Total revenue	563,874
Expenditure (say)	192,422
Net revenue according to this method	371,452

Value of plant 633,970*l.*		
25 per cent. on this	£158,492	
Other allowances	5,814	
		164,306
Value for assessments		207,146

Thus the line of railway is assessed on nearly two-fifths of its gross earnings.

* Evidence of Mr. G. Dods, assessor of railways and canals in Scotland.

The result is, that while the return on the total capital employed in the Caledonian, North British, Glasgow and South Western, Highland, and Great North of Scotland Railways is 4·02 per cent., the percentage of valuation to gross revenue is 27·97 per cent., and to net revenue 55·32.*

The percentage of railway valuation to valuation of all other property is 10 per cent., while the percentage of acreage (20,148) of railways to acreage (20,030,017) of all other property only about one-tenth of 1 per cent.†

This is the method of rating in Scotland, where "means and " substance," which would of course include stock in trade, are, in the case of such companies, included in the assessment. But, nevertheless, the incidence of the taxation on railways in England (including rates and Government duty), notwithstanding that " means and substance " are not ostensibly included in this country, is heavier than either in Scotland or Ireland.

The figures for the year 1867 are given below from Slaughter's " Railway Intelligence " for 1869 :—

	Rates and Government Duty.	Per Cent. to Profit.
	£	
England	1,165,295	6·96
Scotland	114,402	5·44
Ireland	51,051‡	5·20
United Kingdom	1,330,748	6·71

‡ No Government duty in Ireland—rates only.

It now becomes desirable to refer to those charges on local funds which have been thought rather to belong to the imperial budget. The grants by Government in aid of such charges have necessarily to be considered with them.

As fresh requirements have arisen in various directions, such as for police, more efficient schoolmasters in workhouses, and some medical charges, the outlay has occasionally been so great that the property liable to assessment in the places concerned has appeared to be inadequate to meet the burden. Hence arose the necessity of some mode of bringing the imperial exchequer to aid, while endeavouring to avoid endangering the security for economy obtained by the local principle of making those pay who administer the expenditure; and an arrangement for grants in aid has followed.

These, as made at present, do not appear to have proceeded on

* Appendix, No. III. Report from Select Committee on Valuation of Lands and Assessments (Scotland) Bill, 1870.
† Appendix, No. II, ditto.

any systematic principle. Like much modern legislation, they may
have been based on the rough-and-ready method of the "rule of
"thumb" rather than on any more exact arrangement. A more
equitable division might be made by enacting that those expenses,
in the administration of which local knowledge and the desire for
local economy are of little or no avail, or in the incurring of which
local requirements have little or no share, should be regarded as
fit subjects to be separated from the local and placed on the imperial budget.

The subject has not escaped the notice of Mr. Gladstone, who,
speaking on local taxation on 21st February, 1870, in the House of
Commons, remarked, "I am bound to say that it would be very
" wise to arrive at a conclusion with respect to the present assis-
" tance given from the imperial funds to local purposes; to ascer-
" tain whether it is too great or too small; whether given in the
" best manner, and whether or not it interferes with sound prin-
" ciples of administration."

The existing arrangement is open to great objections, with but
few corresponding advantages. A grant made in aid of any branch
of local expenditure, the police, for instance, requires a corresponding inspection, to ascertain that the purposes for which the grant
was made have been fulfilled. This inspection, if slight, cannot be
satisfactory; if complete, involves a system of supervision which
would suffice of itself, to the complete administration of everything
concerned. To revise these assisted charges, and then to place the
whole cost of those retained as of imperial concern on the consolidated fund, would probably result in a considerable economy from
the remedial effects of a more systematic arrangement. The country meanwhile would be spared the great and increasing evils of
divided local jurisdiction. The police force certainly appears to
need a more complete organisation, which could scarcely be effected
without a more direct control from a central authority.

"There are, exclusive of the police of the metropolis and the
" city of London, something like 200 separate forces (in England
" and Wales) acting quite independently, having each local interests
" to serve, subject to distinct local authorities, and unaccustomed
" to co-operate for the furtherance of any common object. It is
" owing in a great measure to this cause that the supervision of
" convicts in England under the Act of 1864 has not been more
" efficient."—Colonel James Fraser, Commissioner of Police, letter
in the "Times," 13th March, 1869.

It must be borne in mind that this needless subdivision involves,
in an economic point of view, an unnecessary number of separate
funds for providing superannuation allowances; doubtless, also, an
unnecessary number of superior officers for so many small detach-

ments ; with other expenses of stations, &c. ; and the waste in the cost of administration involved by so many separate jurisdictions in many ways.   Nor is the confining the career of an efficient police officer of any grade to the narrow limits of a local force in any way desirable.   If a really capable man, he is always on the look out for openings elsewhere; while the system of appointment by the selection of local authorities and testimonials has but little to recommend it.   A broader field, with the larger prizes naturally open in consequence, would be likely to secure the services of a better class of officer, while the chances of immunity now obtainable by the law-breaker among the differences of jurisdiction, would be curtailed or lost.   In both cases economy would probably result.   It is probable that a consolidation of these 200 forces of police would lead to other advantages in administration besides those mentioned by Colonel Fraser ;—a more complete repression of crime, a more complete supervision of vagrants, to mention these points alone, would lead to considerable economical advantages.   To continue this portion of the subject, as an illustration of the wide field still open for improvement, the vast and increasing number of tramps and vagrants may be referred to.   The need of a careful and rigid dealing with this dangerous class of the population is most pressing, and has been made the subject of a special inquiry.*   The numbers of tramps are very differently computed in different returns.   This is alone sufficient to indicate the need of a uniform mode of dealing with such persons.   The following extract from the Report of the Poor Law Board, 1869-70, shows the difference between returns of vagrants made by the police, and those of poor law guardians.   With this statement may be compared the numbers noted in one county of England alone (Hampshire), amounting in 1869 to 26,479.   The individuals of so wandering a class may doubtless be frequently counted over and over again in many differing localities; but the difference in the numbers stated is too great to be accounted for by this explanation only.

" Our attention has been drawn to the great discrepancy between " the number of vagrants, as shown by the returns prepared by the " clerks to the guardians, and summarised by us, and the numbers " given in the returns which have hitherto been issued by the " police.   For instance, the number of vagrants known to the police " were :—

On 1st April, 1867 32,528
        "   '68 36,179

" Whereas the poor law returns showed the number of vagrants

* *Vide*, " Presented by command " [No. 14678], " Reports on Vagrancy, " made to the Poor Law Board by Poor Law Inspectors, 1866."

" to be, on 1st January, 1867, 5,027; and 6,129 on the same day in
" 1868.

" This great difference arises from the circumstance that the
" guardians necessarily confine their return to those vagrants who
" apply to them for relief, while the police authorities include all
" persons known to them as vagrants and tramps, whether sleeping
" in casual wards at the cost of the rates, or in lodgings at their
" own expense. In fact the poor law returns only deal with *pauper*
" vagrants, the police returns with *all* vagrants and tramps."—
" Twenty-second Annual Report of the Poor Law Board, 1869-70,"
pp. xxx and xxxi.

The principles which apply to the regulation of the police
apply with even more force to gaols. No reason can fairly be given
for constituting any penalty inflicted by the Imperial Government a
charge on local taxation. Does the fact that a rogue reared, say at
Cardiff, is captured and convicted at York, render it a fair thing
that the ratepayers of that locality should have to contribute at all
to his maintenance, while he is expiating his offence in the castle or
the city gaol. The offence was against the laws of the country ;
should not the whole of the expense of the administration of those
laws be borne by the country ?

While on this portion of the subject, it is desirable to consider
whether any good reason can be given for the maintenance of both
a city and a county gaol in the same place, or for retaining a distinction between local and imperial prisons. It may be added that a
complete and uniform administration over the gaols of the country
would probably not only lead to some considerable economy, but by
strengthening the hands of authority, conduce to a more efficient
repression of the criminal and vagrant classes.

Though it is most desirable the administration of ordinary
pauperism should rest with the locality concerned, a doubt arises
whether the same reasons apply in the case of lunatics, or those
incapacitated by some bodily defect from gaining a livelihood.

Part of the reasons for keeping the management of the funds
for the relief of the poor in the hands of those interested in the
locality, is that their local knowledge may detect fraudulent imposi-
tions on the poor fund, and in other similar ways promote economy.
In neither direction can these reasons have as much force in the
case of lunatics as of ordinary paupers. "The enforcement of a
" regular test of destitution in all doubtful cases, and a system of
" administration in the hands of the elected agents of the ratepayers
" of a limited area," well said to be the strong points of the existing
system, are of less avail in respect to these cases, which can also be
scarcely properly attended to within the walls of the ordinary workhouse without great additional expense, both in providing specially

trained attendants and suitable accommodation. The presence, too, of idiots or the "fatuous," in the Scotch sense, in the adult wards is highly objectionable. A large asylum, or, could a suitable opportunity be found for it, arrangements for boarding out on the Belgian system, appear to present better opportunities for the management of such cases. Should a reconsideration of local charges take place, this portion of the subject might well be investigated. "It is clearly "an expense which stands on a different footing altogether from "the other items of poor law expenditure."—"Twenty-second "Report of Poor Law Board."

That any of the expenses attending the militia should be reckoned among charges to be defrayed by the county, can only be explained by remembrance of the historical position of that force. As a reconsideration of the whole question of national defence appears probable, it is sufficient to advert here to the fact that the expenses of the volunteer forces of the country (in some respects more "local" even than the militia) have been defrayed without hesitation from the consolidated fund. There can be no doubt that if the militia were of as recent an introduction as the volunteer force, all the expenses entailed by it would be defrayed from the same source, as the latter is.

The payments on account of the Registration Act,—the expenses connected with parliamentary registration and the cost of the jury lists,—also appear to be distinctly expenses incurred for imperial, not for local purposes, and should be dealt with accordingly.

X.—*Other Sources of Revenue than Rates.*

As other means of raising or contributing to a local revenue than the sums raised by rates are within the scope of this work, it is desirable to give some notice of them.

Markets.—The tolls to be raised from this source can never, or at least ought never, to be very high. If these tolls rise to such a scale that they augment the cost of the provisions sold, they amount in fact to an octroi duty, one of the most undesirable methods of raising a revenue that can be devised, from the inequality of the incidence. A tax on provisions falls most heavily on the lowest sections of the poorest classes, and is open to almost every objection which can be raised to a tax. Such taxes must, from their nature, be almost invariably opposed to Adam Smith's first canon of taxation, "that each person ought to contribute to the revenue in propor- "tion to his ability to pay." A tax on coals has the same disadvantages with a tax on provisions, with the additional one that it is a direct tax on all manufactures within its limit as well. Such forms of taxation are fortunately so little known in this country that the opinion of a foreigner, and of a Frenchman, the inhabitant of

a country where octroi duties are of frequent occurrence, is the best
to be cited :—

" Moins grand est le gâteau et plus fortement le fisc le rogne.
" C'est vrai encore et surtout de l'impôt de consommation. Le fisc
" ne tient presqu'aucun compte ni de la qualité ni du prix. Le
" ' petit bleu ' qui empoisonne le maçon ' contribue ' autant que le
" Chateau-Margau dont se délecte l'entrepreneur; ainsi pour la marée,
" les viandes, les liqueurs. Personne n'ignore, de plus, que les
" depenses sujettes à imposition prennent une part autrement large
" sur le budget de la mansarde que sur le budget du premier étage.
" A supposer, par exemple, que les impôts et octrois sur les liquides,
" les comestibles et les combustibles les renchérissent de vingt pour
" cent., cette sur-dépense de vingt pour cent. absorbera peut-être le
" cinquième et au-dela du revenu de l'ouvrier ; elle n'augmentera
" pas d'un vingtième la depense totale du fabricant."—" Le Bilan de
" l'Empire," par M. J. E. Horn. 2ième edition, p. 10.

Tramways.—A small fixed charge may fairly be laid on such undertakings. This may be considered as a rent for the use of the soil
covered by the lines of way, and for the privilege of passage. It might
either be levied as a rent, or as a percentage on the traffic. Taxes on
locomotion should, however, never be sufficiently high as to interfere
with its complete freedom, or in any way to impede the traffic. It
is not probable that any large revenue. can, except in the largest
cities of the empire, be raised from this source. A concession for a
term of years, as in the case of our Indian and most foreign
railways, offers obvious advantages for a fair adjustment of charges
between a municipality and a company offering to make such lines.
The "Tramways Act" of last session gave permission to "local
" authorities " to construct such lines in any part of Great Britain,
and likewise authorised the borrowing money for a period not
exceeding thirty years for the carrying on of the works where the
"local rate " is insufficient. With this object the Metropolitan
Board of Works is authorised to borrow 300,000l. This sum, if
raised, will be levied on "occupiers " alone, while experience shows
that "owners" are the eventual gainers by the improvement in
the value of property which increased facilities for locomotion tend
to produce.

Sewage Farms.—"Sewage farms " have been indicated as probable sources of income to local authorities. In some instances such
undertakings have been already attempted. The scheme in use at
Cheltenham is reported to be in profitable operation. In the existing
state of the question little more can be said than that some of the
projects seem to promise favorably. That a considerable source of
profit exists is obvious ; as also that at present but little use has
been made of it. The sciences of chemistry and engineering will

probably before long find a solution of the difficulties which hitherto
have prevented success.   Meanwhile, the following remarks by
Mr. Corfield do not appear out of place here.

(*a.*) That by careful and well-conducted sewage irrigation,
especially with the application of small quantities per acre, the
purification of the whole liquid refuse of a town is practically
perfect, and has been ensured in cases where it was not at all the
object of the agriculturist; and that it is the only process known
by which that purification can be effected on a large or small
scale.

(*b.*) That by it the value of land is enormously increased—at
least doubled in every instance. That perfectly worthless land,
blowing sea-sand, for instance, can be made in this way to support
large and valuable crops.

(*c.*) That the quantity per acre obtained from all crops is
enormously increased.

(*d.*) That it reduces to a great extent, or entirely renders
unnecessary, the usual amount of artificial manures of all kinds,
by supplying a manure especially adapted, from its complex constitution, for the nourishment of crops, supplying it moreover in a
state of solution; that is to say, in the most readily absorbable
condition, and supplying at the same time that most necessary aid
vegetation, water, by which the value of the manure during the
greater part of the year is almost doubled.

(*e.*) That by it the farmer is rendered almost entirely indepen-
dent of the weather, so that he can be practically certain of his
crops, and, moreover, be able to transplant them as much as he
pleases.

(*f.*) That with all these advantages it is no wonder that whenever sewage has not been wastefully applied it has been found to
pay; and that when its management is more thoroughly understood
it will doubtless be found to be a valuable source of income to the
towns.   In fact, in the words of the Rivers Pollution Commissioners
(1870), intermittent filtration is a costly process with no possibility
of any return; whilst irrigation, although it may in the first
instance require a larger outlay of capital, affords a hopeful prospect
of a return for the capital invested.*

Gasworks.—The profits derived from the gasworks in the hands of
the Manchester corporation, have frequently been cited as an instance
of the advantage to be gained by making such undertakings the
property of a municipality.   Manchester has undoubtedly been
considered benefitted by this arrangement; no less a sum than

* " A Digest of Facts relating to the Treatment and Utilisation of Sewage."—
By W. B. Corfield, M.A.   London : Macmillan and Co., 1870.

477,713*l.* having been paid over for purposes of local improvements
up to 1866. In looking into the matter, however, as a guide for
similar arrangements elsewhere, it has to be remembered that
Manchester presents a very favourable opportunity for such a plan,
in consequence of the large field for operation. The arrangement is
one of long standing in the place. The Manchester gasworks were
transferred to the corporation in 1844. The maximum price of gas
was 6*s.* per 1,000 feet within the limits of the city at that time. This
price was gradually reduced, till in 1865 it was 3*s.* 2*d.* per 1,000
feet; and the profits realised on the capital invested have been
greatly diminished in consequence, although not in proportion
(from 19·78 per cent. in 1844, to 13·20 per cent. in 1866); some
compensation having been found in the greater consumption. The
profits, as in all similar industrial undertakings, fluctuate con-
siderably. In 1867 the balance available for improvements was
diminished to 13,257*l.*, as against 19,516*l.* in the preceding year,
though an increase took place in the consumption of 5·04 per cent.,
and a reduction is stated to have occurred in the illuminating power
of the gas supplied, the price remaining the same as in the preceding
year. The gradual diminution in the balance available for local
improvements appears to have led to a practice which must be
considered an objectionable one, of anticipating future profits as
yet not realised. This arrangement, sanctioned by the city council
(4th March, 1868), though not without some dissentient opinions,
has been continued. At a meeting of the council, 6th October, 1869,
" the further sum of 11,303*l.* 19*s.* 8*d.*, in anticipation of future
" profits," was directed to be paid over for local improvements.
The price of gas in Manchester appears to be about the same as in
some other towns nearly similarly situated. Thus, at Sheffield,
where the works (1869) were in the possession of a Company, the
price was 3*s.* 3*d.* per 1,000 feet. The general tendency appears to
be in favour of authorities purchasing gasworks, to judge by the
number of such arrangements which have recently been made. There
are other reasons besides those of profit which lead to this result.
Some advantages will presumably be obtained by the local authorities, as at Manchester, but it is probable that, unless under very
favourable circumstances, considerable profits cannot be looked
for.

Waterworks.—Waterworks appear to be in general less profitable
to corporations than gasworks. So much depends on the condition
in which such works are maintained; the state of the " fittings " in the
premises supplied, a proper allowance in the accounts for depreciation and other points in the working, that a comparison between one
place and another requires to be made with care. The position of
the metropolitan water companies appears to be exceptional, and

is, therefore, not referred to further here. According to the "profit "and loss account" of the Manchester Corporation Waterworks for the year ending 31st December, 1868, after setting apart 12,316*l*, for the sinking fund, a suitable but not excessive proportion on a cost of works nearly approaching to two millions, the deficiency on the year's working was 919*l*. 2*s*. 7*d*.

At Liverpool, where the works also belong to the corporation, the results do not appear to be much more satisfactory. By the published statement of the ordinary receipts and expenditure of the Liverpool water account for twenty-one and three-quarter years, 1848-69 ; the net result as regards profit appears to be only 6,353*l*. 3*s*. 9*d*. This being the net profit in the course of the period stated on an invested capital larger than that at Manchester, more than 2,100,000*l*. According to the abstract of the ordinary receipts and expenditure at Liverpool for the period mentioned, it is obvious that, though a small net profit was, as mentioned above, 'the result of nearly twenty-four years' trading, there were many years included in that period during which the working did not produce a profit at all, but on the contrary, the balance was on the other side of the account. The depreciation fund appears on the whole to be smaller at Liverpool than at Manchester.

The rates charged at Bradford and those at Dewsbury, works belonging to municipalities, the latter a joint concern with Batley and Heckmondwike, may be cited as instances of the charges made in smaller manufacturing towns. At these places, as also at Manchester and Liverpool, a water *rate* is made on all rateable property in aid of the charges (this rate being understood generally to represent the original outlay on the concerns which is thus charged on the occupiers), a water-rent being levied besides on all consumers. At Dewsbury, the water rate for the current year is 4*d*. in the pound. At Bradford it is 2*d*. in the pound. The annual charge for water on a house of the yearly rent of 13*l*. at this last place are as follows :—

		£	*s*.	*d*.
Water rate, 2*d*. in the pound	....	-	2	2
„ rent	....	-	19	6
		1	1	8

By way of comparison with these charges, the scale in use at Yarmouth, in Norfolk, where the waterworks belong to a company, may be cited. According to these, a house of a similar rent with that instanced above (13*l*. per annum) would be charged 15*s*. 8*d*. per annum. These rates likewise include a water-closet—not permitted without extra payment at Bradford, and charged there

5*s.* per annum — bringing the total charge in that place to 1*l.* 6*s.* 8*d.* per annum for similar accommodation to that charged 15*s.* 8*d.* a-year at Yarmouth. As there are differences of conditions in circumstances of the works at the places above named, which, it may be supposed, prevent their being suitable for purposes of comparison, it is desirable to add that all are on the constant supply system, but that, while all the works belonging to the corporations named are worked on the principle of "gravitation," the one belonging to a company is a "pumping scheme," thus involving extra cost. The difference of charge to the smaller consumer may be also pointed out by observing that the "company" charges commence on a lower scale, without a rate, than those of the "corporations" with a rate beyond. It does not appear, therefore, that the consumer in the instances given is benefitted, as far as price is concerned, by the works being in the hands of the corporations. But price is only one element among many in this question. There are many and weighty reasons against waterworks being conducted as trading concerns only. These reasons are best indicated by the following extract from the report of the Medical Officer of the Privy Council, 1870:—

" It seems to me that the public is hitherto very imperfectly " protected against certain extreme dangers which the malfeasance " of a water company, supplying perhaps half-a-million of customers, " may suddenly bring down upon great masses of population. Its " colossal power of life and death is something for which till recently " there has been no precedent in the history of the world ; and such a . " power, in whatever hands it is vested, ought most sedulously to be " guarded against abuse. I venture to submit that the penalty of " 200*l.*, which the Metropolis Water Act imposes for a violation of its " provisions, is utterly incommensurate with the magnitude of the " public danger, which a lax administration of the law represents ; " and it is certain that in 1852, when this statute was enacted, the " state of science did not yet enable the legislature to know, as it " must now know, that a water company distributing sewage-tainted " water may, in a day, take hundreds of lives."—*Dr. John Simon.*— From " Twelfth Report of the Medical Officer of the Privy Council, " 1869." The remarks of Mr. H. C. Beloe (2925, Evidence before Select Committee), of the reduction of insurance rates in Liverpool, in consequence of the corporation waterworks, is very noteworthy.

It must be remembered that where water and gas are already in existence they are valuable properties, which the municipalities can only acquire on equitable terms like any other purchaser of the stock or shares in such companies. The municipality is presumably even less likely to obtain the properties at a lower price than any other purchaser for many obvious reasons.* The money, if the properties are bought, must be borrowed, and the credit of a well-managed company is almost as good as that of the best organised municipality. This is readily tested by the rate of interest which each has to give in borrowing on debenture. The difference is not likely to exceed one-half or three-quarters (10s. or 15s.) per cent. in favour of the muncipality, against which must be set the drawback of the absence of individual interest on the part of the managers. Some profits may arise from extension of works, but these will require time for their development; while there will always remain the great disadvantages arising from fluctuations in the managing body. As town councils and local boards are at present constituted, it is to be feared that among the conflicting claims of the local interests of a ward, or the petty squabbles of municipal politics, the greater or less fitness of candidates for the management of water or gasworks are likely to be overlooked or disregarded.

The charges of the works belonging to companies are likewise in many cases so restricted by local Acts of Parliament, that it is not probable that in such instances any considerable reduction in price would be experienced by the inhabitants if the works were taken over by the municipality.

As water supply was especially included within the scope of the present inquiry as a source whence local revenue might be derived, it is considered that the details given above on this subject, and on gas supply as well, will not be considered irrelevant. Without some such details it is scarcely possible to give even an outline of the peculiar bearings of this part of the question. There are many reasons, as indicated above, besides financial considerations, which render it desirable that municipalities should acquire such undertakings. Some profit may be looked for, which will naturally extend with the growth of the population, and the consequent extension of the works ; but in most cases, and under most circumstances, this is not likely to be large. No fair sources of profit, however, should be overlooked.

XI.—Incidence of Local Taxation.

In London, the case of the ratepayer seems, at present, to be a peculiarly hard one ; a poor's rate of 1,683,750l. is levied, 2s. 1d. in the pound, with an amount of all other rates of 1,526,844l., forming a total rate of 4s. in the pound. Of this latter sum, a portion of about a million a year, according to Return 430, is due to general district and lighting rates.

---

* Vide the Dundee Gas Companies' case. The companies claimed to receive annuities of about 20,000l. per annum in payment of their works, and received at the rate of 8,600l. per annum.

	£
General district and lighting rates being	981,140
The sewers rate	280,005
Main drainage	198,113
Other rates	36,006
	1,495,264

These figures, however, are very far from representing the total amount of expenditure in the metropolis. According to Mr. Goschen's return, this rises for the year 1868 to the enormous sum of 8,010,000*l*. The receipts exceeded this sum, and were as follows:—

£	
3,470,000	raised by rates.
390,000	by dues, tolls and fees.
580,000	,, rents and sales of property.
400,000	,, Government subvention.
290,000	,, miscellaneous receipts.
3,100,000	,, loans.
8,230,000	

As the sewers rate and main drainage rate are raised, generally speaking, for permanent improvements, it appears that a tax of nearly half a-million a-year is levied for these purposes on the householders of London, whose interest in the dwellings they inhabit is usually less permanent than that of any other class of occupiers.

The want of a complete system of local government in the metropolis is well known; while the attempts to improve on the existing state of affairs have been many, though hitherto unsuccessful. Some remarkable hints may be obtained from Mr. Pownall's evidence. The paper handed in by him to the "Select Committee" of 1870, of the county expenditure of Middlesex, shows that while a taxation of 172,127*l*. is annually raised for county purposes, the quarter sessions have real control only over 4,103*l*. These last remarks refer, strictly speaking, to the expenditure of Middlesex, not of the metropolis.

In a city so vast as London, containing a population so varied in character, in education, in property, a good system of local government presents peculiar difficulties. The recent elections for the Metropolitan School Board give a hope that means may eventually be found to induce the metropolitan ratepayer, to take a share in the local government of the largest city in Europe.

The late Sir John Thwaites gave very strong evidence in favour of dividing the "municipal, but not parochial, rates between the

" owner and occupier in equal shares, considering that the owner
" greatly benefits by the expenditure, and every reletting improves
" the beneficial interest that the owner has in obtaining a larger
" rental."—Evidence, Select Committee, 4027.

The parochial rates do not, according to this witness, improve
the value of property, while, as indeed is obvious, "it is greatly
" improved in value by the expenditure for metropolitan improve-
" ments." Sir John Thwaites most strongly objected to the view
" that rates come from the pocket of the owner." Being asked
" whether, if, by any regulation the rates at present paid by the
" occupier were divided equally between the owner and the occu-
" pier, the occupier would gain an advantage by such a rearrange-
" ment?" The answer was, "Yes, he would be relieved from that
" moiety of the burden, and I think that would for many years
" be an accepted charge on property, and that they (the owners)
" would not seek to cast it, ought not to have the power to cast it,
" on their tenants."

A stronger expression of opinion could not well be found in
favour of a division of rating between owner and occupier. The
compromise suggested seems a fair one: that the division should
extend to the municipal, but not to the parochial rates, and be
confined in fact "to taxation for metropolitan improvements,"—
to the taxation which tends to the permanent improvement of
property.

The question as to the incidence of taxes as between owners
and occupiers gave rise to a considerable conflict of opinions from
those who gave evidence on the subject before the select committee
of last year, as it has done whenever the subject has been considered and discussed. This discrepancy of opinion marks with a
something approaching to precision the division between the rural
and the urban ratepayer.

"There can be no doubt whatever that a portion of the rates
" does ultimately fall upon the owner; what is in dispute is, the
" amount which falls upon the occupier. It is held by some that all
" rates ultimately fall upon the owner; by others, that a large por-
" tion is borne in fact, as well as in form, by the occupier."*

The fact that the occupier pays the rate himself, not unnaturally
leads him to the idea that he bears the burden entirely, and alone.
But in a vast number of cases, this is an erroneous impression. The
owner bears his share in the diminished rent, which the property
produces, where the rates are excessive. This state of things holds
good in those hirings in which the demand is not in excess of the

* "Proceedings of the Select Committee on Local Taxation, 1870," p. xvi.
Some selections from the evidence are given, Appendix, No. VI.

supply. Here the broad distinction between house property and
property in land, between the property which can, and that which
cannot, be increased in quantity at pleasure appears at once.
Though the tenant of a house is usually to a considerable extent
confined, as to the general situation, to one locality in the choice of his
dwelling, yet his choice as to a house itself is by no means so
limited. In these isolated cases where the whole, or nearly the
whole of the house property of a town is in the hands of one man, a
practical monopoly takes place. The house landlord may, if he
chooses, say, "pay the rent I require, or you shall not be able
" to avail yourself of the advantages of living in my town." But
these extreme cases are few ; and in the vast majority of towns, there
is almost as great a choice of landlords as of houses.

Still, in many instances, the landlord has a very considerable
power over the tenant whenever the lease terminates. Where the
house to be let is in a neighbourhood which possesses any special
advantages, it has a kind of monopoly value. It becomes a question
of calculation,—of what Adam Smith would have termed " the
" higgling of the market,"—whether it is a greater loss to the
tenant of a house in a good situation to leave his shop or his office,
and move elsewhere, or to submit to pay a higher rental. He
would yield the point, and pay higher rates, as well as a higher
rent, rather than move, if he thinks it worth his while. Against
such contingencies no legislation can guard. When considerable
local improvements have been made, and the amounts needed for
the purpose borrowed on security of the rates, on the usual provision that a certain proportion of the principal of the loan as well
as the interest should be defrayed by the proceeds of a rate levied
yearly, there can be little doubt but that, at the end of the term,
if the prosperity of the country remains then the same as now, and
the locality continues in the same request, the landlord would, as
each house became vacant, be able to exact from the hirer the old
rent, plus the rate which would have terminated, the amount of the
rate having through lapse of time become incorporated with the
hiring value of the house. Thus the improvement of the locality
would be effected with the tenant's money, to his immediate as well
as abiding prejudice.

Another objection sometimes made to the levying so large a
portion of local taxes on house-rent is that the impost thus becomes
a tax on a particular description of property, to the exclusion of the
other means the householder may possess. But this is not in reality
a valid objection. " No part of a person's expenditure," as Mr. Mill
has well expressed the case, " is a better criterion of his means, or
" bears on the whole more nearly the same proportion to them. A
" house tax is a nearer approach to a fair income tax, than a direct

" assessment on income can easily be ; having the great advantage,
" that it makes spontaneously all the allowances which it is so diffi-
" cult to make, and so impracticable to make exactly, in assessing
" an income tax : for if what a person pays in house-rent is a test
" of anything, it is a test not of what he possesses, but of what he
" thinks he can afford to spend." — " Principles of Political
" Economy," J. S. Mill, p. 405. Fourth edition.   Proper allowances for premises employed for trade purposes, or let as lodgings,
are essential to the fair apportionment of a house tax, as well as a
careful adjustment of the proportion of the burden levied for permanent improvements between owner and occupier.   When these
points have been attended to, the tax seems as fair an impost as
can be made.   It will be a matter of regret if it is abandoned as a
branch of imperial taxation in this country.

As Mr. Goschen stated, in his speech on the 21st February, 1870 :
" Certain rates were imposed to obtain some actual benefit, and being
" spread over a number of years, were in their nature reproductive.
" In the case of a great and permanent improvement calculated to
" last a hundred years, a man with a twenty years' lease would not
" only have to pay the interest on the loan contracted to defray the
" cost of that work, but to contribute towards the payment of the
" principal as well; while at the end of the twenty years the owner
" would step in and take the whole benefit."   To obviate this, the
most equitable mode of proceeding would be to follow the plan
recommended by the Report of the Select Committee, and apportion
such rates between the owner and tenant.

The existing plan in Scotland is to divide most rates equally.
This may be desirable where the plan has existed from time immemorial.   A large and sudden increase in the taxation of a particular
form of property is open to many objections, and would probably
be very unjust to a vast number of the persons concerned.   The
method followed in Liverpool, when the corporation waterworks
were established, may be cited as almost the only instance in England
of a division of a large amount of rating, in modern times, between
landlord and tenant.   Here the division of rating, as mentioned in
Mr. Beloe's evidence, though only the moiety of one rate, amounted
to a property tax of 1¼ per cent., which represents 3d. in the pound.
The half of one rate, however, is a very different and much smaller
charge than the half of all the rates, a division which, it is probable, would not have been assented to with equal readiness by the
house owners.   Other witnesses who gave evidence before the
Committee seem to have thought, and with some appearance of
probability, that a large addition of taxation to the owner might
lead, at the commencement at all events, to some retaliating charge
to the occupier.   It may hence be desirable that the division should

not be made according to the Scotch scale, but on some intermediary plan, allotting, say one-third to the owner, two-thirds to the occupier. It might also be considered whether in certain districts, and especially in the case of owners of ground-rents in towns, a fixed scale of division might not be objectionable; and, as an alternative, an apportionment according to the circumstances of each case or district might be made with advantage by a jury, by commissioners, or by some enlargement of the powers of the " General Assessment " Sessions." For the better guidance of procedure, certain fixed limitations, that the proportions should not exceed certain limits (those given above for example) in either direction—either to the owner or the occupier—would be desirable.

It is now needful to refer to the alteration in the incidence of local taxation which has, in this country, followed the altered proportions of the two main divisions of real property. The great and progressive increase, especially of late years, of houses and other real property "other than land " was referred to before.*

According to the returns obtained on the motion of Sir M. H. Beach (in 1868), though the total local taxation of England and Wales in the years 1863-65 was nearly equally divided between the cities and towns (including the metropolis) and the counties, the incidence of the taxation was far heavier in the urban than in the rural districts. Though these returns were, from the manner in which they were drawn up, imperfect and incomplete, yet they tend to demonstrate the general fact that the towns are far more heavily rated, in proportion to wealth, than the rural districts.

In order to endeavour to trace this subject further, a series of tables is given. For these tables the Returns 283, of 1864, " Population, Electors, &c.," and 454 of 1870, " Income and Property " Tax," have been employed as a basis, and the rates as given in Returns 497—497 I, and 430, 1870, apportioned as closely as the method in which the returns are made out will admit. The boundaries of the parliamentary cities and boroughs of England are in many instances very irregular and ill-defined. A borough is frequently divided into many parishes, of which parts only are sometimes included; occasionally situated in more than one union, in more than one district for various purposes of rating, and in more than one county.† The boundaries of the borough have been followed out according to their parliamentary definition; and the population (the Census of 1861 being taken as the basis throughout

---

these returns) afforded some clue in the more difficult cases. It has thus been endeavoured to give in these tables as close a statement of the incidence of the present local taxation as the form in which the existing returns are made out will admit. Although, from the circumstances mentioned, it has not been possible to present an absolutely accurate statement, it is considered that these tables give as complete a chart of the local taxation of England as is possible at the present time, and that the general results which are there shown may be safely relied on.

The amount levied in England for all rates, as given in the " Summary for Counties, Return 430," has been divided in Table A between the respective heads of Poor's Rates (Col. 1), Purposes of Local Government (Col. 2), Local Improvements (Col. 3). It becomes obvious that the rate in the pound raised for poor rates varies far less in proportion to the rateable value than the rates for government and improvements. This is brought out more clearly in Tables C and F, in which the rates are arranged in proportional order according to the counties. And the incidence of the rates both on the towns represented in Parliament in each county, on the counties both without the towns represented and including them, is likewise shown.

Table B groups these figures together in districts as nearly coincident in extent with those given in the reports of the Poor Law Board, as the form in which the returns are made out will allow. A note to this table compares the incidence of the poor rate in other districts on the rateable value, with its effect on the basis of the income tax assessment. It will be seen that similar results with those mentioned in the preceding paragraph appear also when counties similarly circumstanced as to population, occupation of inhabitants, and like social conditions, are grouped together.

The difference between the rural and the town districts, both as to incidence of tax and the purposes for which levied, deserves attention. Table C shows, in Col. 1, the incidence of all rates in the counties of England after deducting the rates levied in the towns represented in Parliament in 1862. Middlesex and Surrey are not included, as, from the exceptional wealth of these counties, and the manner in which the town and country districts in them are intermingled, no satisfactory basis could be attained for this purpose, so as to admit of a comparison with the other counties. Wales is given for the principality, the boundaries of the places represented being so ill-defined that it was found impossible to separate each borough or district, except in very general terms, from the surrounding population. Col. 4 of the same Table (C), gives the similar details of rating on the towns represented in each

county named. Col. 7 contains tho total rating in tho counties,
with tho towns included. It will bc observed that the towns thus
grouped aro rated higher than the "counties." Cornwall is an
exception to this. In Cornwall several of the boroughs may bo
described as " geographical expressions," and the character both of
the property and of the inhabitants within and without the electoral
boundaries do not widely differ from each other.

These details are arranged in Tables C and F according to the
maximum amount levied in each case. There appears considerable
doubt whether the amount of rates described as levied in the
towns of the county of Lancaster can be safely relied on.*   A
local return, kindly supplied from Liverpool, shows results con-
siderably different from those traceable in Return 497. Several
of the rates included in this return do not appear named in the
columns of the parliamentary return. A note is therefore marked
against Liverpool and Lancaster, but the general totals have not
been altered, as it does not seem certain that the particulars in
the local return corresponds exactly with those in the return made
to Parliament.

Tables H, I, and K contain the position in 1868, as to all rates,
of the towns in England returning members to parliament in the
year 1862, with the exception of the metropolitan boroughs. These
places have been selected as forming as fair a guide to the urban,
distinguished from the rural population, as circumstances admit.
The difficulties attendant on the drawing up these tables have been
mentioned previously. Table H gives the total rate in the pound
of all rates, for each place named. The poor rates are given in a
similar manner in Table I. Table K subdivides the rates for local
government and for purposes of improvement and health.

The general results are as follows :—

Table H, the places named pay a total rate of 3s. 11¾d. on tho
rateable value for all rates.

The summary in Return 437 (1870), dividing the local taxes in
1868 between rural and town unions, states the total taxation of
the town unions as 4s. in the pound. The method followed in the
return made by the Poor Law Board does not exactly correspond
with that adopted in this paper, but the coincidence is so close as
to show that the general results may be relied on. The same places
average for poor rate 1s. 8¾d. in the pound, while other rates aro
8¾d. for local government, 1s. 5½d. for improvement rates. England
generally, as shown in Table A, averages 1s. 6½d. in the pound for
poor relief.†

* " Lancaster," appears to bear a rate of 5s. 6½d. in the pound on towns
represented when thus amended.

† The estimate in Mr. Goschen's report is 1s. 6d.

It is hence obvious that the poor's rate is less onerous in the towns than the other rates : though, as shown in Tables C and D, the towns are rated for *all* rates more heavily than the counties. Mr. Goschen's investigations show the same results.

" Applying, therefore, the historical test geographically, the con-
" clusion is, that purely agricultural counties are less heavily rated
" than formerly, though, owing to their enormous hereditary poor
" rates, many of them remain high in the list, while the manufac-
" turing and metropolitan counties show greatly increased rates,
" partly owing to increased expenditure for poor relief, but in great
" part to the vast sums which have been spent on town improve-
" ments.

" An examination in more detail of the counties themselves
" confirms the principle here laid down in a remarkable degree.
" The more urban the union in any county, the higher does the
" rate per pound for all rates rise, as compared with the county
" average.

" In most counties it is almost sufficient to pick out the union
" in which county towns and other towns are situated to find the
" union where the highest rates prevail. There are some natural
" exceptions, such as the fen districts, where heavy expenditure for
" drainage purposes raises the rate ; but the following statement
" shows the general result (all rates being taken into considera-
" tion) :—

	Average Rate for County.		Union of Highest Rate.		
	s.	d.		s.	d.
Berks	3	4	Reading	4	9¾
Chester	2	9¾	Chester	5	2¼
Derby	2	4	Derby	3	6¼
Essex	3	5	Colchester	5	5¼
Hertford	3	1	Hertford	3	8¼
Huntingdon	4	7½	Huntingdon	3	3¾
Leicester	2	7¼	Leicester	4	4¾
Northampton	2	11¾	Northampton	4	3¼
Northumberland	2	8¾	Newcastle	4	3¼
Nottingham	3	-¾	Nottingham	5	7½
Oxford	3	1	Oxford	3	11¼
Southampton	3	10½	Southampton	7	-¼
Worcester	2	8¼	Worcester	4	6¾
Wilts	3	2¼	Salisbury	7	10

" Other counties show the following result:—

	Number of Unions.	Average Rate of County.	Unions of Highest Rate.		
		s. d.		s.	d.
Bedford	6	3 6	Woburn	4	4
			Luton	2	2¼
			Bedford	3	7
Devon	20	3 2¾	Plymouth	6	10
			Stoke Damerell	6	4¾
			East Stonehouse	5	–
Dorset	12	3 4½	Poole	4	10¾
			Blandford	3	9¾
			Bridport	3	9½
Durham	15	2 8¼	Sunderland	4	5¾
			Gateshead	4	–
Gloucester	17	3 4	Bristol	5	3
			Clifton	4	–
Kent	29	4 8¾	Greenwich	6	1¾
			Dover	5	2½
			Woolwich	4	10¼
			Canterbury	4	8½
			Gravesend	4	6½
			Maidstone	4	5¼
Monmouth	6	3 6½	Newport } Pontypool }	3	7¾
Norfolk	23	3 1	King's Lynn	7	2¼
			Norwich	7	1
			Yarmouth	7	–
Stafford	16	2 8	Wolverhampton	5	–½
			Stoke-upon-Trent	4	8½
Surrey	21	4 5½	Rotherhithe	5	9½
			St. George's, Southwark	5	1¼
			Camberwell	5	–½
			Lambeth	5	–
			Croydon	4	4¼
Warwick	13	3 1¾	Coventry	4	10½
			Birmingham	4	6¼
Yorkshire (E. R.)	10	2 7¾	Kingston-upon-Hull	4	2½
Yorkshire (W. R.)	37	3 7½	Leeds	7	7½
			Sheffield	5	2¾
			Bradford	4	11¾
			Dewsbury	4	4

" It is unnecessary to quote the cases of Lancashire and Middle-
" sex, of which so large a portion is urban. The foregoing tables

" appear to prove conclusively that, as in looking to the counties as
" units, the great increase in the aggregate of local burdens was
" found to be in manufacturing and urban counties ; so, in looking
" to the unions composing each county the urban unions are subject
" to by far the the heaviest taxation."—" Report on Local Taxa-
" tion, 1870."

By Table K, it is shown that in the towns of England
(the counties are found in Tables A and G), local government
causes a far slighter taxation than local improvement. The local
government rate for the towns averages only in the aggregate*
$8\frac{3}{4}d$. in the pound, while local improvement reaches† $1s$. $5\frac{1}{2}d$. in
the pound, involving a taxation not far short of the poor's rate.
The local government rate cannot, however, be taken as in any way
representing the real cost of local government.   The large sum
derived from the corporation estate at Liverpool in aid of the
borough fund may be cited as an instance.   Similar property and
tolls, such as harbour dues and river dues, are applied to a like
purpose in many other boroughs.—*Vide* " Macclesfield," *supra*,
p. 145.

The large amount levied for improvement rates, about 1,700,000*l*.
for the towns, nearly 500,000*l*. for London, must be regarded as a
tax levied on occupiers for the ultimate benefit of owners, principally of house property.

The pressure of rates on seaport towns attracted Mr. Goschen's
notice.   A table in his report exhibits this point very clearly.   It
will have to be borne in mind in considering this point that several,
probably most, of the places named derive an income, generally
employed in abatement of local charges, from charges on shipping.
Without this assistance the rates would fall even more heavily.

" Another interesting fact, which a careful examination of the
" returns of the amount of rates brings out in strong relief, is that
" seaport towns, compared with the average rating in England, bear
" a remarkably heavy share of local burdens.   The following table
" may be of interest in this respect :—

---

* On the other hand, England generally, Table A. averages $1s$. $\frac{1}{4}d$. in the
pound for local government, and only $9\frac{1}{4}d$. in the pound for local improvement.

† Table C shows how greatly the local improvement rates vary in proportion
between one county and another.   While the poor rate varies only from 37 to 100,
proportionally (Table F) ; and local government varies in nearly the same ratio,
36 to 100 ; local improvement rates vary from 5 to 100.

Unions containing Seaport Towns.	Rate.		Average Rate of County.		Unions containing Seaport Towns.	Rate.		Average Rate of County.	
	s.	d.	s.	d.		s.	d.	s.	d.
Bideford	4	2½	3	3	Newcastle-upon-Tyne	4	3¼	2	8¾
Birkenhead	4	5¾	2	9¾	Newport	3	7¾	3	6½
Boston	3	6½	3	-¼					
Bridport	3	9½	3	4½	Plymouth	6	10	3	3
Brighton	5	6¼	4	-¼	Poole	4	10¾	3	4½
Bristol	5	3	3	4¼	Portsea Island	6	4¾	3	10¼
Cardiff	3	9½	3	8¼					
Cardigan	4	8¾	4	4¼	Southampton	7	-¼	3	10¼
					Sunderland	4	5¾	2	8¼
Gravesend	4	6½	3	8¾	Swansea	6	7¼	3	8¼
Holyhead	5	2¾	4	6					
					Weymouth	3	8	3	4½
Ispwich	4	7½	2	11½	Whitehaven	2	11¾	2	1
					Whitby	3	8¾	2	4
King's Lynn	7	2½	3	1	Woolwich	4	10¼	3	8¾
Kingston-upon-Hull	4	2½	2	3¾					
Liverpool	4	4¼	3	5	Yarmouth	7	-	3	1

Local taxation has sometimes been considered as unequal taxation, it therefore becomes desirable to inquire where this inequality exists. Table D gives the incidence of the poor's rate according to population. The position of some of the agricultural counties in this table is very noticeably high. It is desirable to refer to Table L, in which the proportion of the assessment under Schedule A is given for certain counties of England for the years 1803 and 1866-67. Their position at the earlier date is given to show that the condition of these counties in this respect has remained nearly uniform, nothwithstanding the great changes in the relative proportions of the various descriptions of property in the country indicated in Table M. It will be observed that although, as shown by these latter tables, real property "other than land" is now the bulk of real property in England, the agricultural counties have still maintained their position as to the relative proportions of wealth, calculated according to the *numbers* of the population. Hence, it will be seen that although the agricultural districts are all rated high for poor's rate, and high for all rates in proportion to their population, they stand equally high in the scale of property, and consequent ability to bear taxation.

In prosecuting this inquiry it now becomes desirable to ascertain what the effect of levying the poor's rates on an income tax assessment would be. To show the result completely, the income tax has been calculated as a rate in the pound on the rateable value, and also an estimate has been made of the effect of a levy of the poor's rate on a property and income tax assessment. Tables F and G contain the results which the income tax, under Schedules A, B, D, E, 1862, would show if, instead of being raised in the present manner, it were levied as a tax on rateable value for the counties of England. The result shown by this table is remarkable. The income tax is usually considered an equal charge, as far as the comparison of one place with another is concerned, but if it were levied, like the poor rate, on the rateable value, it would appear to show nearly as great inequalities as the existing local taxation.

In Table F, the result of levying the poor's rate on the assessments under Schedules A, B, and D, is shown. Such an assessment would bring income (Schedule D, representing trades and professions) largely into the account. But, as shown in Table F, the results differ very slightly indeed from a poor's rate levied, as now, on the rateable value. Even including Middlesex, the results (taken on the basis of representing by 100 the maximum rate) vary from 33 to 100, while on the rateable value they vary from 37 to 100. The agricultural counties generally, with the exception of those in the north, are very high on the scale in both instances. The industrial and manufacturing counties find their position slightly lower with an "income tax," than with a "rateable value," assessment.

It appears clear that as regards the poor rate, neither an equalising of taxation, nor a gain to those counties which appear heavily weighted, would be caused by an alteration in the mode of assessment from a property to an income tax basis. The counties generally in the two columns on Table F maintain their relative position with great closeness. Individuals in each place would find their burthens lightened or increased—but to the community at large, taking district by district, the alteration would be but trifling. On many accounts a great and permanent increase to the income and property tax is exceedingly to be deprecated. This subject is so important that a further space will be devoted to its consideration.

A persevering effort has continually been made in late years to charge certain large items of expenditure, which have hitherto been defrayed from local taxation, on the consolidated fund. The poor's rate has been one of the charges thus named, and the income tax pointed to as the best method of bringing "means and substance" in the Scotch sense into contribution. To place the poor's rate on the general taxation of the empire, and to add to the income tax in proportion — would, as stated at p. 36, require that tax at one

stroke to be doubled—a 10*d.* or 11*d.* income tax would probably
have to be levied in ordinary years. This, too, only at the existing
rate of expenditure for the relief of the poor.

It cannot be doubted, also, that such a step, removing the advantage of local supervision, would tend at once to a large increase of
the expenditure; while the imposition of a high rate of income
tax is known, unfortunately, to lead to increased evasions and
fraudulent returns. In reply to such a proposal the following
remarks, from the reports of the Commissioners of Inland Revenue,
appear not inappropriate; bearing in mind the observations of the
same commissioners (p. 29, Report 1870) of the "demoralising
" influence, so destructive to the character of a people, of the
" habitual and successful evasion of law, whether fiscal or other-
" wise." It appears desirable to give some of the instances named.

" The claims to compensation which have arisen out of a recent
" extensive demolition of houses in a certain district by the Metro-
" politan Board of Works, have given the usual evidence of the
" frauds which prevail in returns under Schedule D.

" Proceedings have been taken in the Court of Exchequer in a
" large number of cases, and in none have the defendants ventured
" on resistance ; but the penalties recoverable are not even sufficient
" to compensate the revenue for the duty evaded, and consequently
" inflict no adequate punishment for the frauds committed.

" The following are selections from the cases of surcharge.
" Case I :—

		£		£
1865.	Return	250 ;	assessment	400
'66.	„	400 ;	„	400
'67.	„	1,000 ;	a surcharge to	1,900

" was confirmed on appeal to the district commissioners.

" The excuse which this person offered, in order to obtain a
" mitigation of the penalties, was that he had no idea what his
" profits really were.

" A surcharge was made on a large amount in order to compel
" the parties to appeal and produce their accounts.

" On proceedings being taken, the defendants attempted to justify
" themselves by stating that *their returns bore fully as large a pro-*
" *portion to their actual income as the returns made by their competi-*
" *tors, and others in trade;*" and that to have made true returns
" *would have been in effect to penalise themselves.*"

" Of course, if this were a solitary instance of the kind it would
" be eminently illogical to build any argument upon it, but your
" lordships are aware that, as an invariable consequence of claims
" for compensation, where the actual profits of trades or professions
" are divulged, we find the income tax returns largely deficient.

" And, moreover, this is not confined to any particular class, trade,
" or profession; we find the same practice prevailing among legal
" practitioners, when, on the abolition of their exclusive privileges
" in some particular court, they have to make good their claims to
" your lordships; we find it on all occasions of large demolition of
" shops and warehouses for public purposes, in every variety of
" trade, and we find it in great public companies and in firms whose
" business is almost a national concern, from its magnitude and
" world-wide reputation; we therefore think that we may venture to
" generalise upon the facts which the most recent occasion of com-
" pensation cases has furnished.

    " Those facts are, that 40 per cent. of the persons assessed had
" understated their incomes to such an extent that a true return
" would give an addition of 130 per cent."—" Twelfth Report of
" Commissioners of Inland Revenue, 1869," p. 19.

    It must also be remembered that the experiment has been tried.
That income has at times been brought into contribution for local
rates both in England and in Scotland;* that in England the
method has been completely, and it is to be hoped, finally abandoned.
A short historical outline of the effect of rating stock in trade in
one particular branch of industry in England is not out of place
here.

    The original intention of the statute of the 43rd of Elizabeth,
the basis of English legislation on the subject, has been construed to
include stock in trade.   The impolicy of the practice, the anomalies
which it would involve, the difficulties which were experienced in
carrying it into effect, have caused the plan to fall into desuetude.
The following remarks on this subject, from the Report on Local
Taxation of 1843, put the matter in the clearest light.   As it may be
held that, were the custom universal in the United Kingdom, such
a migration of an industry from one district to another, as appears
to have been the result of the partial infliction of the impost therein
described, would be impossible; it is sufficient to reply that a
migration of an industry, and the attendant capital, from Great
Britain to a colony or to some foreign country, is scarcely attended
with more difficulties now, than a migration from one district of
England to another, a hundred years ago.

    " The practice of rating stock in trade never prevailed in the
" greater part or England and Wales.   It was, with comparatively
" few exceptions, confined to the old clothing district of the south
" and west of England.   It gained ground just as the stock of the

---

* The practice, though now stated to be frequently discontinued, was continued
to so recent a date, that the late Lord Campbell is said to have been on one occasion
assessed upon his salary as Lord Chancellor, as forming a part of his " means and
" existence."—Evidence before Select Committee, A. 111, *Mr. J. Lambert.*

" woolstaplers and clothiers increased, so as to make it an object
" with the farmers and other ratepayers, who still constituted a
" majority in their parishes, to bring so considerable a property within
" the rate. They succeeded by degrees, and then followed upon
" their success a more improvident practice in giving relief than
" had ever prevailed before in England. It was in this district,
" and at this time, that relief by head-money had its origin, and
" produced its most conspicuous effects in deteriorating the habits
" and depreciating the wages of the agricultural labourer. When
" the practice of rating stock in trade was fully established in this
" district, the ancient staple trade rapidly declined there, and with-
" drew itself still more rapidly into the northern clothing districts,
" where no such burden was ever cast upon the trade. Whether
" this transfer of business was in any way aided by the imposition of
" the burden of the poor rates, county rates, highway rates, and
" other rates upon stock in trade in the one district and the exemp-
" tion in the other, cannot perhaps now be distinctly proved; but
" it is undeniable that the operation must have been in effect a
' discriminating tax of very considerable amount against the trade
" of the one district, and therefore proportionally in favour of the
" trade of the other. In both districts the industry was of ancient
" growth, but hitherto the southern district had had the advantage;
" for the natural and acquired advantages of the two districts are in
" most respects such as rather to have favoured the southern
" district; the density of the population, the possession of an indi-
" genous raw material of a good quality, the proximity to the
" ancient and important seats of commerce, London and Bristol, the
" possession of valuable coal fields, the investment already effected
" of a capital greater than had ever, until very recently, been
" invested in any branch of English manufacture, unlimited
" resources available for new investments in the accumulated wealth
" of the district, above all, the possession of unequalled skill for
" which, and for a superior kind of produce, it even yet retains a
" character, were advantages apparently sufficient of themselves to
" have enabled the district to have maintained at least an equality
" with its rival in the north."—" Report of the Poor Law Commis-
" sioners on Local Taxation (1843)," p. 37.

XII.—*Concluding Remarks.*

The conclusion appears clear. The present mode of raising a
tax for local purposes by an assessment on the rateable value
appears to be in the main a fair one. Certainly as equal in incidence as the existing property and income tax. The inequality that
exists resides, not in the mode of raising the revenue, but in the
application of the sums raised.

Taxes for the relief of the poor, for local government, for general government, for local improvements; taxes levied for very different objects are raised in the same manner on properties for the most part belonging to one set of persons, and occupied by another. There are very material distinctions between the application of the various sums raised under the general description of local taxes. There are very material distinctions between the interests of owners and occupiers in the same property which the existing arrangements do not notice. The purely local should be completely separated from the imperial taxes. When this is completed there will yet remain to carry out the principle of no taxation without representation; to abolish all *ex officio* authority; to give the county ratepayer a voice in the administration of the sums to which he contributes. There will yet remain to bring the owner, whether of land or of house property, the person ultimately most concerned, into council, to decide what charges should be placed on his property. Lastly, it appears desirable to divide at least the rates levied for purposes of improvement, if not all rates, the preferable plan, between the owner and the occupier. The half rating system for agricultural assessments, was advocated as far back as 1869, in a paper read before the London Farmers' Club by Captain F. L. Dashwood, and the advantages of the closer supervision from landlords, when personally interested, was very clearly shown.

Leasehold property presents some points of difficulty; but the recommendation to exempt the owners of such property for a certain number of years, and then to allow them to add a fair proportion of the fresh tax to their rents, seems an equitable solution of the difficulty.

It is possible, as named above, pp. 58—64, that some reduction of local burdens may be obtained by local governing bodies administering or leasing out waterworks, gasworks, rights of way such as tramroads, by a careful utilisation of sewage, and so forth. But the auxiliary sums to be raised by these means must in most cases, of necessity be slight in amount, though careful management will not disdain any fair source from which assistance may arise.

It is probable that reduction in local taxation must be looked for in a different direction. Administration affords the widest field.* The economy which it cannot be doubted would result by concentrating a complete control of the expenditure under the eyes of the

---

* Modern statutes have rendered England an aggregate of parishes. The parish is our territorial *unit*; but the ancient *units* were the common law divisions of townships and wards, or other civil jurisdictions of an analogous nature; and from the neglect of the ancient principle many inconveniences arise.—*Sir F. Palgrave* on "Corporate Reform."

ratepayers; the economy to be effected by systematic management, by a reduction in the number of duplicate offices, in the expenses of collection, by the adoption of a well organised local goverment, can hardly fail to be very considerable.* A well organised system of local government is, however, beyond the scope of this book. It is most likely that the fact of uniting all local charges in one general rate, with a complete and uniform system of accounts for the United Kingdom, would speedily attract so general an interest to the subject, that a revision, and it is to be hoped an amelioration, of the existing legislation would shortly follow.

---

* Areas for Local Taxation.

NOTE.—" By the aid of the Home Office blue books and the Poor Law Board's " reports, the following list of the local jurisdictions of England and Wales has " been constructed :—

14,880 parishes severally raising poor rates.
   65 quarter sessions severally raising and administering county and police rates.
    1 corporation of the City of London.
 220 town councils severally raising and administering borough and police rates.
    1 Metropolitan Board of Works.
 648 poor law unions.
 379 highway divisions under 12 and 13 Vict., cap. 35.
 305   ,,   districts under 25 and 26 Vict., cap. 61.
  53 South Wales highway districts under 23 and 24 Vict., cap. 68.
 124 towns improvement commissions.
 700 local boards under the Public Health Acts.
  49 commissions of sewers.
 157   ,,   drainage and embankment.
 280 parishes under Lighting and Watching Act, 3 and 4 Wm. IV, cap. 60.
  40 metropolitan vestries and district boards.
 330 burial boards.

18,232 total jurisdictions taxing real property.

" We are not certain within half a dozen places whether the numbers ascribed to " towns improvement commissions and to local boards are correct. Both bodies " appear to be in a state of flux. Three or four years ago more than 200 of the " latter suddenly presented themselves without warning in the local taxation volume "'of the Home Office. The aggregate of the list above exhibits 18,000 and more " jurisdictions possessing the power of taxing rateable property for local purposes. " Two exceptionally important corporations are included—the City of London and " the Metropolitan Board of Works. The former renders no public accounts of its " income or expenditure. But local taxes are also raised by tolls and dues through " the following means :—

 958 turnpike trusts.
  75 bridges and ferries.
  44 markets and fairs.
 114 harbours.
   2 the Trinity House and the Northern Lighthouses.

1,193 total jurisdictions levying tolls and dues.

" Adding this total to the former, we have more than 19,400 taxing bodies, leaving " out of view 460 parishes raising church rates according to the last return— " omitted here since church rates are destined to complete extinction shortly."— From " Pall Mall Gazette," 13th October, 1871.

APPENDIX I

—

" THE properties made expressly liable by the statute of Elizabeth are:—

1. Lands.	4. Propriation of Tithes.
2. Houses.	5. Coal Mines.
3. Tithes Impropriate.	6. Saleable Underwoods.

" 1st. ' Lands' are understood to include profits derivable from the use or sale of the body of the soil itself; from the growing produce of the land, and from improvements of the land. But although it thus includes quarries, clay-pits, gravel-pits, mineral waters, salt springs, &c., it is construed in the statute of Elizabeth not to include mines, it being held that the express mention afterwards in the statute of 'coal mines' shows that it was the intention of the statute not to rate other mines.

" The word ' land,' as it includes generally the renewable produce of the land, would have made all kinds of wood and timber rateable. But it was held upon the same principle as that by which all mines but coal mines were exempted, that the express mention in the statute of 'saleable underwoods' exempts all wood and timber not coming under the denomination of saleable underwoods. The word ' lands' is construed to include improvements of lands by roads, bridges, docks, canals, and other works and erections not included under the term 'houses.' If the principle of construction, by which it was held that the mention of 'coal mines' and of 'saleable underwoods' exempted all other mines and all other woods and timber, had been extended to this class of properties, it would have been held that the express mention of 'houses' would have exempted other erections and buildings not coming within the description of houses; such a construction, however, has rarely been contended for, and has not been adopted.

" 2nd. ' Houses.' This term in practice is apparently admitted to include all permanent erections for the shelter of man, beast, or property. It did include places of worship, other than episcopal churches, until the 3 and 4 Wm. IV, cap. 30, exempted places of worship, so far as they are used for religious purposes, or for Sunday or infant schools, or for the charitable education of the poor.'

" 3rd and 4th. ' Tithes Impropriate ' and ' Propriations of Tithes.'

" The rent charges payable instead of these tithes were declared by the 6 and 7 Wm. IV, cap. 71, to be subject to all kinds of rates in the same manner as the tithe itself had theretofore been.

" These two species of tithe, together with the tithe of the efficient incumbent, comprise all the tithe known in England; but it has never been held that the express mention of these two species has the same effect as the mention of coal mines and saleable underwoods, to exempt from the tax the unmentioned tithes of the efficient incumbent.

" 5th. ' Coal Mines.' The effect of the express mention of coal mines in exempting all other kinds of *mines* from the rate has been adverted to. The exemption extends to all mines, even of matters usually quarried, as limestone mines and clay mines. On the other hand, if materials usually got by mining are taken from the surface of the earth, or by excavations not denoted by the word ' mines,' the occupier of the land is rateable for the profit as a profit of the land. When coal is procured from the surface, or by operations or by excavations not denoted by the word ' mines,' it is generally treated as a subject of the tax; being perhaps rated as ' land,' not as coal mines.

" But a series of recent decisions has curiously broken in upon the exemption of mines. It is now held that if the owner of a mine lets it, reserving as rent a portion of the produce unwrought, he is rateable for that produce as occupying land. Thus the law now is, that an owner who works the whole mine, and takes all the produce, is exempt as to the whole, and that a lessee is exempt as to the whole;

that the owner is also exempt for his rent if reserved in money or even in the wrought or smelted produce of the mine; but that if the reservation be of a portion of the produce of the mine, he is rateable for that portion.

"6th. *Saleable Underwoods*.' The effect of these words has been much disputed; they are understood to include wood, of whatever nature, cut down periodically, and shooting again from the same stem to be again cut in like manner. The use of the word 'saleable' is understood to exclude such underwoods as are to supply the land with estovers and fuel, or serve for shelter to young wood, or for ornament or other purposes of the estate.

"These words operate by construction to exempt, as before observed, all other kinds of wood and timber. Saleable underwoods were made liable to the tax, and other woods and timber exempted, probably in accordance with the rest of the policy of the Act of Elizabeth, which appears to have intruded in all cases to charge the occupiers of property, and to exempt the interests of the owners. Saleable underwoods were almost invariably farmed out, while wood and timber was reserved by the landowner. It seems to have been thought that the tax could be laid on the occupier without affecting the owner. Although this conclusion is not consistent with the more accurate views of modern times in relation to rent and taxation, a great variety of passages in the reports show that such a belief did prevail extensive, and for a long period subsequent to the passing of the statute of Elizabeth."—"Report on Local Taxation (1843)," pp. 31—33.

APPENDIX II.

NOTE referring to the inconvenience of legislating on the poor's rate without taking into consideration all other local rates:—

"In considering these instances, it is right that it should be borne in mind that there is no other subject upon which the existing legislation is in fact so certain, or upon which Parliament and the public generally are so accurately informed, and so intelligibly and directly interested, as the present subject of taxation. In respect of most other rights conferred, and obligations imposed by the legislature, a certain latitude of enjoyment and of obedience is inevitable, and much of the effect of the law may safely be made to depend on the general sense which people have of their reciprocity of interest; every person subject to an obligation at one moment, being equally entitled in his turn to the enjoyment of the right conferred, and to benefit by the obligations imposed on others for securing its enjoyment. In matters of taxation, the recognition of the burden of the obligation is always easy, but the perception of the reciprocal benefits to be enjoyed is less easy and less general. Precision of expression is universally felt to be necessary, when every man is to be compelled to make definite sacrifices, and submits to the law with reluctance. This precision of expression is also most easily attained, because the liabilities are dependent on simple circumstances, and are not subject to be modified or rendered intricate by complicate private arrangements, and are measured by arithmetical (that is, by easily definable) proportions; the whole of the law is put into operation through the ministration of special functionaries, whose information, when new legislation is contemplated, is always officiously offered, or readily to be procured. No subject could therefore be selected, of which the matter is in so defined a form as the present, or so clearly expressed, and so little likely to afford examples of ignorance in Parliament of the existing state of the law at the time when they legislated. Nevertheless, even here, the instances are sufficiently numerous and striking to illustrate the prevailing fashion of legislation.

G 2

" Scarcely anything can be more material than the declaration of the *persons* or *properties* to be rendered liable to a tax. Yet there is hardly an instance in any modern act, where the intention has been to impose the tax on the basis of the poor's rate, in which the purpose has been legally or unambiguously effected, not because there is the smallest difficulty in effecting it, but merely because the draughtsman dispensed himself from looking at the statute of the 43 Eliz., and Parliament and the public had no ready means of checking the draughtsman while the Bill was in progress. Thus the highway rates are made taxes on the property without apparently following the person. The same defect applies to the Lighting and Watching Act, 3 and 4 Wm. IV, cap. 90, sec. 9, with the addition of a positive confusion as to the persons liable, caused by the use in section 33 of the term ' owners and occupiers of land,' terms not reconcileable with those of the statute of Elizabeth. In other cases the error is reversed, and the property is left to be inferred, and the persons only fixed, and this often with gross inaccuracy; thus in the Militia Rate Act (43 Geo. III, cap. 90, sec. 42), the persons described as liable are the ' inhabitants of the parish, &c., according to the rate made for the relief of the poor,' the strict effect of which is to omit both the chief persons and chief property, subjects of the poor rate, namely, the occupiers of the real property and the tithe owners, and to charge only the persons liable to poor's rate in respect of stock-in-trade. The defects of the Act for the General Sewers Tax, in this respect, have been partly described above. The County Rate Acts, unlike the Militia Rate Act, refer to the ' occupiers of estates and property, and omit inhabitants as well as parsons and vicars (55 Geo. III, cap. 51, sec. 12); while, as regards the property to be rated, the confusion is extraordinary, being described for parishes where poor rates are made, by terms inapplicable to the property liable to poor's rate, while for extra-parochial places where no poor's rate is made, the liability of property is strictly identified with the liability to poor's rate. The same confusion is adoption, to the county rate for shire halls, to the rate for burying dead bodies, and apparently to the rate for lunatic asylums. Not to make the enumeration fatiguing, reference may at once be made to the proper titles . . . to show that in this the most important provision in relation to every tax, the confusion is almost universal.

" After the declaration of the liabilities of persons and property, one of the subjects about which Parliament would be most vigilant, would be the provision for *remedies* against an illegal tax, and against irregularities in its imposition. To take the most recent instances of legislation, the 3 and 4 Vict., cap. 88, sec. 8, assumes that a right of appeal is given against the police rate in places within the county, and affects to extend the same right of appeal to detached places; but no such appeal as the one assumed to exist does exist, and the appeal supposed to be conferred by reference is, therefore, a mere illusion. In the majority of cases no remedy at all is given against the tax, or it is given by some equally illusory reference, or is so imperfectly constructed as to be worse than nothing, in as far as it deludes people into litigation and its expenses, without affording them protection. It would be again quite tedious to repeat the instances.

" Of still greater importance, however, is the subject of *accountability* of those who have the collection, custody, and distribution of a tax. Yet is this subject sometimes wholly forgotten, as in the workhouse building rate, the survey rate, the rate for gaol fees, the constables' rate, the militia rate, the burial-ground rate, the hundred rate. Sometimes the existence of the liability to account is left doubtful, as in the General Sewers' Tax Act. Sometimes it extends only to a part of the funds, or a part of the persons in respect of which it should be provided, as in the case with the Lighting and Watching Rate Acts, omitting overseers; the Sewers' Rate Acts, omitting the commissioners; the County Rate and Borough Rate Acts, omitting justices and borough councils, all through the series of rates imposable on the counties, hundreds and boroughs.

" These instances, though a very small part of what the single subject of local taxation affords, and selected only from the most important heads of the subject, will be more than sufficient to show how entirely fortuitous our legislation is upon a subject in itself the most intelligible, and capable of most accurate definition.

" It thus occurs that an accumulation of original and substitute provisions co-exist for the same purpose. The co-existence of the sewers rate, and of the general sewers tax is apparently an instance of this ; the co-existence, in the Tithe Commutation Acts, of two distinct sets of provisions for determining the boundaries of properties and parishes, the first of which ought to have been repealed, is another ; the co-existence of three discordant sets of provisions for the inspection of poor's rates is another ; the co-existence of an original appeal to quarter sessions, of an original appeal to special sessions, and of an appeal from thence to quarter sessions, is another ; the co-existence of three general accounts, and of a multitude of special and occasional accounts by overseers, is another ; the co-existence of two appeals to the same sessions against the accounts of overseers, is another ; not to mention multitudes of like instances applying to most of the other rates.   Every such instance is at least a useless incumbrance to the statute book, and to every compilation ; and causes a perpetual embarrassment to the public, to functionaries, to courts of justice, and to Parliament itself.

" One example of an insufficient repeal is presented by the abrogation of the liability to pay poor's rate in respect of personal property (Appendix A, Poor's Rate, par. 74).   This liability is only by implication repealed in the case of some other rates, viz., the county rate, *semble* in extra parochial places, par. 31, 70, 74; *semble*, and *qu* as before, par. 22, 71 ; the county rate for shire halls *semble* and *qu*, as before, par. 32, 62 ; the rate for burial for dead, *semble* and *qu* as before, par. 32, 62 ; the hundred rate where there is a county rate, subject to the same question as county rate, par. 32, 33, 62 ; where there is no county rate or similar fund, then as poor's rate, par. 30, 44; the borough rate, when paid out of poor's rate, par. 30, 66a, 68, 70 ; but *qu*, as above, when made as county rate, par. 32, 62, 66, 71; the borough watch rate, when paid out of poor's rate, par. 66.   The liability is left in full force in others, viz., in the constables' rate, par. 30, 70, 74 ; the highway rate, par. 30, 59, 74; the lighting and watching rate, par. 30, 59, 70 ; the militia rate, but *qu*, par. 30, 74.   The church rate, par. 59; the burial ground rate (*qu*) ; in other cases it is doubtful whether the liability is repeated or still exists, viz., as to the gaol fees rate, par. 30, 71 ; the police rate, par. 32, 62 ; the borough rate, par. 30, 32 ; the borough watch rate, when not paid out of poor's rate, par. 66, 71."—Note to " Report on Local Taxation, 1843," p. 3.

APPENDIX III.

—

COMPARATIVE taxation in the United Kingdom and in New York State.

From the " Economist" newspaper, 1st June, 1867.

" A recent number of the ' New York Commercial Chronicle ' contains the following statement :—

" The Comptroller of this State has written a letter to the Chairman of Ways and Means Committee of the Assembly, showing that a State tax of over *one* per cent. will be required this year if the measures now before that body are adopted. It may not be uninteresting for the legislature, in connection with this letter, and while they are considering the propriety of so largely increasing our burdens, to examine the extent of the imposts of 1866, when the State rate was only about five mills per cent.   The necessary data will be found in the following comparative aggregate of taxes—State, county, and town—levied in 1860 and 1866, prepared from the official reports :—

Aggregate Taxes Levied in New York State in Years 1860 and 1866.

Tax.	1866.	1862.	Increase.
	$	$	$
State tax	7,369,000	4,376,000	2,993,000
School tax	1,148,000	1,064,000	84,000
County ,, ...	22,316,000	10,738,000	11,578,000
Town ,, ...	9,734,000	2,776,000	6,958,000
	40,567,000	18,954,000	21,613,000
Equal to a levy per dollar of valuation of .... }	25½ cents	13⅜ cents	12 cents

" If anybody desires to know how much more the camel's back will bear, the following comparison between 'tax-ridden Great Britain' and our own State, will furnish food for reflection :—

Internal Taxes, 1866, of Great Britain and Ireland (Population 30,000,000).

	£		$
Excise	20,000,000	=	100,000,000
Stamps	9,550,000	=	47,750,000
Taxes	3,500,000	=	17,500,000
Property tax	6,000,000	=	30,000,000
	—		195,250,000
County and local	18,500,000	=	92,500,000
	—		287,750,000

" The following are the figures for New York State also in 1866 :—

Internal Taxes New York State (Population 4,000,000).

	$	$
United States internal revenue .... }	—	49,000,000
State taxes	7,369,000	
County and local	33,200,000	
		40,569,000
		89,569,000

" Giving as the proportionate results :—

$9·59 per head in Great Britain and Ireland.
$22·75   ,,   New York State.

" We must confess that we are somewhat startled by this result. We were aware and have often said that the taxation in the States was high, but we were not prepared to find that in New York State the assessment is more than *double* the rate paid in this country. Nor would the introduction of the customs' revenue at all lessen the disadvantageous nature, as regards New York, of the result as it stands. On the contrary, the American tariff is far more oppressive and more obstructive than with ourselves."

Appendix IV.

"Reform, or, if necessary, suppress vestries—give property its proper influence—take from justices all power to interfere in the concerns of the poor, and leave the rest to the self-interest of the parties. This system has been found to be completely successful in Scotland, and there is no room or ground for thinking that it would be less so in England. In Scotland the affairs of the poor have been managed by the heritors (proprietors) and kirk sessions. The latter, to which the administrative details have always been confided, consist of the ministers and elders of the different parishes; the elders uniformly almost comprising some of the leading proprietors and most respectable inhabitants. The decisions of the heritors and kirk sessions have not been interfered with by justices, nor even by sheriffs, and have been reviewable only by the Court of Session, which is very chary of interference. In consequence of this arrangement the most vigilant economy has prevailed in all that relates to the treatment of the poor; and while real want has been very sparingly relieved, no encouragement has been afforded to sloth, imposture or misconduct. It is not owing to any superior discernment or ' hard heartedness ' on the part of the Scotch, but to the different mode in which relief has been administered, that the abuses so prevalent on one side the Tweed are unknown on the other. Hence, though the reason of the thing had not been sufficient to prove that the committing the administration of the poor laws to a properly constituted parochial body would suffice to eradicate every abuse, the example of Scotland should have been held as decisive."—Note xxiv to " Smith's Wealth of Nations," p. 596, by *J. R. McCulloch.*

Appendix V.

"Twenty-first Report of Poor Law Board." " The Metropolitan Poor Act, 1867." " Metropolitan Common Poor Fund." " Circular Letter from the Poor Law Board to the Board of Guardians in the Metropolitan District."

" Poor Law Board, Whitehall, S.W.,

" 11*th April,* 1868.

"I am directed by the Poor Law Board to remind the guardians that by section 69 of ' The Metropolitan Poor Act, 1867,' it is provided, that certain expenses incurred after the 29th day of September, 1867, by the several unions and parishes within the metropolis for purposes connected with the relief of the poor, shall be repaid out of a fund, called ' The Metropolitan Common Poor Fund,' to be raised by contributions to be assessed by the board upon those unions and parishes, according to the annual rateable value of the property therein comprised.

" The expenses which are to be repaid are the following :—

" (1.) For the maintenance of lunatics in asylums, registered hospitals, and licensed houses, and of insane poor in asylums under the Act, except such expenses as are chargeable on the county rate.

" (2.) For the maintenance of patients in any asylum specially provided under the Act for patients suffering from fever or small-pox.

" (3.) For all medicine and medical and surgical appliances supplied to the poor in receipt of relief by guardians under the Act, or any of the Poor Law Acts.

" (4.) For the salaries of all officers employed by the guardians in and about the relief of the poor, by the managers of district schools under 'The Poor Law Amendment Act, 1844,' and by the managers of asylums under the Act, and also the salaries of the dispensers and other persons employed in dispensaries under the Act, provided the appointments of the officers have been sanctioned by the Poor Law Board.

" (5.) For compensation to any medical officer of a workhouse affected by the determination or variation by the Poor Law Board of a contract respecting medical relief in the workhouse, or for compensation to any officer of a union or parish who may be deprived of his office by reason of the operation of the Act.

" (6.) For fees of registration of births and deaths.

" (7.) For fees for and other expenses of vaccination.

" (8.) For maintenance of pauper children in district, separate, and licensed schools.

" (9.) For relief of destitute persons certified by the auditor, and provision of temporary wards or other places of reception approved by the Poor Law Board, under the Metropolitan Houseless Poor Acts of 1864 and 1865.

" H. Fleming, Secretary."

Appendix VI.

Extracts from the evidence before the Select Committee of the House of Commons on Local Taxation, 1870.

Rates will fall on Occupier.

" 538. I think that the rates will always be made to fall sooner or later upon the occupier."—*Mr. T. Taylor.*

Rates fall on Owner.

" 774. The rates fall upon the owners of the property, according to my view."
—*Mr. H. A. Hunt.*

Rates.   Owner would Clear Himself.

" 1276. Could you state what difference you think it would make to the owner and the occupier if the tax was imposed on the one or the other ?—I do not think it would be any pecuniary benefit whatever to the occupier. I believe that if the owner had to pay half the rate, he would be sure to recoup himself, whenever there was a rearrangement of the rent: in all probability he would make it safe in this way; I believe the average rates are about 3s. 4d. in the pound in England and Wales, and, if he were to pay half, which would be 1s. 8d., in all probability he would say to the occupier, in order to make myself safe, I shall charge you 2s."—
Mr. C. S. Read, M.P.

Rates on Income Tax.

" 1347. Which do you think would be the best mode of getting contributions from property to local rates; to charge half the rates upon the income tax, or to charge half the rates on the owners of land ?—To charge half the rates upon income tax, most certainly, if general property was to contribute."—*Mr. C. S. Read, M.P.*

Permanent Improvement Paid by Occupier.

" 475. That which is most distinctly a permanent improvement, and which will last for generations, is still paid for by the occupiers at the time?—I suppose even with waterworks, the expenses of repairs and all things considered, the theory has been that those works do not really endure for more than a certain time."—*Mr. Tom Taylor.*

How the Owner Benefits.

" 4029. Your evidence so far goes to the point of that which is spent in the improvement of the metropolis; not money spent in the discharge of burdens such as the poor rate and others?—It is quite clear that in the one case the property of the owner is greatly improved in value by the expenditure for metropolitan improvements, but in the other case, in the expenditure for the relief of the poor, property is not improved."—*Sir J. Thwaites.*

Occupier Pays.

" 4043. Do you assent to the view that it is fair to take the whole of the rates falling upon a house as paid by the occupier of that house?—I think, as a general answer, I believe that that is mainly so; the occupier does pay the rates."

" 4050. That is one of the grievances that I suggest this remedy for, namely, that they are seeking practically to cast the burden upon the occupier by covenants. Let us take any one of the large proprietors in this metropolis, the Duke of Bedford or the Marquis of Westminster, or any of the large proprietors. Supposing leases were granted for fifty years, twenty of which are expired, would anyone suppose that those lessees, at the time when those leases were granted, in which they covenanted to pay the sewers rate, for example, could have contemplated the expenditure, or the especial charge which has been cast on that rate of 3d. in the pound for main drainage purposes? It is quite clear that it never entered into the consideration of A and B, contracting twenty years prior to that imposition by Parliament; and this, therefore, is cast upon the occupier, and he has to pay it, notwithstanding the agreement into which he has entered."—*Sir J. Thwaites.*

Effect of Legislation on Rent.

" 3211. Have you met with many complaints among the tenants of Wiltshire, and those that you have had most to do with, with regard to the increase of rates?—Yes, I may illustrate my own case particularly. I hold my farm upon a lease for sixteen years: the expenditure for rates, until the Union Chargeability Act came into operation, was about 75l. a-year. I am the sole occupier of the parish, I should tell you, except the clergyman, who has a small portion, and the woods belonging to the landlord. The expenditure, as I have said, was about 75l., until the Union Chargeability Act came into operation, and it is now something like from 170l. a-year to 180l. I am paying rather more than 100l. a-year more than I contemplated when I took my farm in 1858."—*Mr. E. P. Squarey.*

Increase of Rates falls on Occupier.

" 3404. Who do you think has borne the increase in the local burthens, as far as your experience goes?—The increase, after the buildings are erected, necessarily comes out of the pocket of the occupier."

" 3409. Assuming that the local taxation increased, you say that either the occupier must pay you more rent or you would stop building?—Yes, or we must get the land at a cheaper rate."

" 3410. Would not that last alternative be the most likely of the three?—My impression is the contrary, because as the population increases the demand increases, and then that always increases the value of land."

" 3 441. Would you say, without hesitation, in the case of house property, the occupier is more interested in the taxation than in the case of land ?—Certainly, as a broad principle."—*Sir S. H. Waterlow.*

Principle of Division of Rates.

" 2979. I think that if they carried out the principle which I sought to introduce into the Bill of 1867, namely, that half the rate should be levied from the owner and half on the occupier, it would have checked the propensity for extreme improvements."—*Mr. H. C. Beloe.*

Application of Principle of Division.

" 3138. Can you tell the Committee anything about the drainage rates of Kent and Sussex ?—No, I only refer to them to illustrate the principle which I would apply.   In the drainage rates of Kent and Sussex, over the Romney Marshes and the levels of that district generally, and the estuaries which flow up into Kent and Sussex, the rule usually is that the scots, as they are termed, that is to say, the cost of maintaining the banks, cleaning the ditches out, and seeing that the waterway is kept in proper order, are borne up to 2s. 6d. per acre by the tenant, and any surplus beyond that is borne by the landlord."—*Mr. E. P. Squarey.*

Effect of Union Chargeability Act.

" 3166. Who would have the power of throwing the greatest number of people upon the rates, the owner or the occupier ? the occupier is a much larger employer of labour than the owner, is he not ?—Yes, but under the Union Chargeability Act I do not think that that feeling operates in the remotest degree with the employer of labour, or with the landowner."—*Mr. E. P. Squarey.*

Occupier Pays the Rates.

" 3375. You would therefore, I presume, not be able to admit that in those cases the rates are paid by the owners of the land ?—Confining myself strictly to those properties as illustrations, I consider that the occupier undoubtedly pays the rates."—*Sir H. S. Waterlow.*

Owners Endeavour to Avoid Rates.

" 2739. In Reading, when there is a new street made, are the paving and lighting met out of the rate, or by the owners of the adjoining property ?—We have had some little difficulty about that ; we adapt it as best we can to the circumstances ; but our principle is that, before we take to a new street for the purpose of paving, the owner should place it in a proper state and condition for a road : he avoids it if he can ; he tries to get it thrown on the public rates as soon as possible, and we have to watch him in that respect.   Say that a man has got a piece of ground for building ; he forms a street, and sells it off into lots of land for building houses, and then he will leave the road to take care of itself."—*Mr. Thomas Rogers.*

Half-surplus to Owner.

" 3130. Do you think it would be a fair arrangement that the landlord should pay one-half of the rates, and the tenant pay the other half ?—Yes, I think that one-half the increase beyond the average is an idea that strikes me as being the fairest way of meeting the difficulty."—*Mr. E. P. Squarey.*

Rates on Owner.

" 2721. The rate ultimately falls on the owner ?—Yes, it must in effect, no doubt : in that sense it would ; that is to say, the owner would certainly get so much less rent for a house."—*Mr. Thomas Rogers.*

Appendix VII.

Taxation in Holland:—

When the taxes which affect the industrial classes are increased, it would seem as if that increase must either immediately fall wholly on profits or wages, or partly on the one and partly on the other. But it generally or rather uniformly gives at the same time such a stimulus to industry and economy as seldom fails to countervail at least in part its depressing influence. And when it is not wholly countervailed in the way now stated, the pressure of the additional taxes, by affecting the condition of the labourers and adding new strength to the principle of moral restraint, assists in replacing them on their old footing.

But whenever taxes become so very heavy that their influence cannot be defeated by increased economy and industry, it becomes most injurious. The oppressiveness of taxation was in truth the principal cause of the lowness of profits in the United Provinces during the last two centuries, and of the decline of their manufacturing and commercial prosperity. Notwithstanding the severe and laudable economy of her rulers, the vast expense incurred by the republic in her revolutionary struggle with Spain, and in her subsequent contests with France and England, led to the contraction of an immense public debt, the interest and other necessary charges on which obliged her to lay heavy taxes on the most indispensable necessaries.[*] Among others, high duties were laid on foreign corn when imported, on flour and meal when ground at the mill, and on bread, when it came from the oven. Taxation affected all the sources of national wealth, and so oppressive did it ultimately become, that it was a common saying at Amsterdam, that every dish of fish brought to table was paid once to the fisherman and *six times* to the State! Wages being necessarily raised so as to enable the labourers to subsist, the weight of these enormously heavy taxes fell principally on the capitalists, and profits being, in consequence, reduced below their level in other countries, the prosperity of Holland gradually declined, her capitalists choosing rather to transfer their stocks to the foreigner than to employ them at home. " L'augmentation successive des impôts, que les paymens des intérêts et les remboursmens ont rendu indispensable, a détruit une grande partie de l'industrie, a diminué le commerce, a diminué ou fort altéré l'état florissant où etoit autrefois la population, en reserrant chez le peuple les moyens de subsistance."[†]—" Principles of Political Economy," by *J. R. McCulloch*, pp. 470 and 471.

---

[*] In 1579, at the Union of Utrecht, the interest of the public debt of the province of Holland amounted to only 117,000 florins; but so rapidly did it increase, that in 1655, during the administration of the famous John de Witt, the States were compelled to reduce the interest from 5 to 4 per cent., and yet, notwithstanding this reduction, it amounted in 1678 to 7,107,000 florins!—See " Metelerkamp, Statistique de la Hollande," p. 203.

[†] " Richesse de la Hollande," tom. ii, p. 179. This work is full of valuable information. The author (M. de Luzac) mentions that the Hollanders had in 1778, about 1,500 millions of livres (62 millions sterling) in the public funds of France and England. See also, as to the taxation of Holland, a " Memoir on the Means of Amending and Redressing the Commerce of the Republic," drawn up from information communicated by the best informed merchants, and published by order of the Stadtholder, William IV, Prince of Orange, in 1751. This 'Memoir' was translated into English, and published in London in the same year. It has since been reprinted by Lord Overstone.

Appendix VIII.

Report of Select Committee of the House of Commons on Local Taxation, 1870.

The Select Committee appointed to inquire and report whether it is expedient that the Charges now locally imposed on the Occupiers of Rateable Property should be divided between the Owners and Occupiers, and what changes in the constitution of the Local Bodies now administering rates should follow such division ;—Have considered the matters to them referred, and have come to the following Resolutions, which they have agreed to report to the House :—

1. That your Committee, without pledging themselves to the view that all rates should be dealt with in the same manner, are of opinion—

(a). That the existing system of local taxation, under which the exclusive charge of almost all rates leviable upon rateable property for current expenditure as well as for new objects and permanent works is placed by law upon the occupiers, while the owners are generally exempt from any direct or immediate contributions in respect of such rates, is contrary to sound policy.

(b). That the evidence taken before your Committee shows that in many cases the burden of the rates, which are directly paid by the occupier, falls ultimately, either in part or wholly, upon the owner, who, nevertheless, has no share in their administration.

(c). That in any reform in the existing system of local taxation it is expedient to adjust the system of rating in such a manner that both owners and occupiers may be brought to feel an immediate interest in the increase or decrease of local expenditure, and in the administration of local affairs.

(d). That it is expedient to make owners as well as occupiers directly liable for a certain proportion of the rates.

(e). That, subject to equitable arrangements as regards existing contracts, the rates should be collected, as at present, from the occupier (except in the case of small tenements, for which the landlord can now by law be rated), power being given to the occupier to deduct from his rent the proportion of the rates to which the owner may be made liable, and provision being made to render persons having superior or intermediate interests liable to proportionate deductions from the rents received by them, as in the case of the income tax, with a like prohibition against agreements in contravention of the law.

2. That your Committee have examined many witnesses, and received at their hands very conflicting opinions as regards the proportion in which the burden of rates at present falls relatively on owners and occupiers.

3. That in the event of any division of rates between the owner and occupier, it is essential that such alterations should be made in the constitution of the bodies administering the rates as would secure a direct representation of the owners, adequate to the immediate interest in local expenditure which they would thus have acquired.

4. That justices of the peace should no longer act *ex-officio* as members of any local board in which such direct representation of owners has been secured.

5. That the great variety of rates levied by different authorities, even in the same area, on different assessments, with different deductions, and by different collectors, has produced great confusion and expense; and that in any change of the law as regards local taxation, uniformity and simplicity of assessment and collection, as well as of economy of management, ought to be secured as far as possible.   .

6. That the consolidation into one rate of all local rates collected within the

same area is a matter of great importance, and that your Committee concur in the Resolution of the Select Committee on Poor Rates Assessment, 1868, which recommended one consolidated rate, viz., "that a demand note should be left with each ratepayer on the rate being made, stating the amount of the requisitions, the rate in the pound for each purpose, and the period for which the rate is made, the rateable value of the premises, the amount of the rate thereon, and of each payment of the instalments of the rates."

7. That whilst it is necessary to make provision for limiting as far as practicable the disturbance of existing contracts, it would be, on many grounds, undesirable, and almost impracticable, to extend the exemption of property held under leases from the operation of the proposed changes until the expiration of such leases.

8. That the exclusion of the owners of property held under long leases from the right of voting for local authorities, after the proposed changes had taken effect in respect of other property, would lead to much inconvenience and confusion, while on the other hand it would be inadmissible to allow them to vote unless they acquired an immediate interest in the rates.

9. That the difficulties of the case would be equitably met by exempting the owners of property held under lease from the proposed division of rates for a period of three years, and by providing that after the expiration of that time the occupiers of such property should be entitled, equally with all other occupiers, to deduct from the rent the proportionate part of the rates to which the owner may become liable, power being given to the owner at the same time to add to his rent a sum equivalent to the like proportionate part of the rates, calculated on the average annual amount of the rates paid by the occupier during the three years above referred to.

10. That by the terms of the reference to them your Committee were limited to the question of the division of the charges on rateable property between the owners and occupiers, and what changes in the constitution of local bodies administering rates should follow such division ; and they have consequently been precluded from entering upon the inquiry of the relations of local and imperial taxation, and the nature of the property liable to the same.

11. That your Committee are of opinion that the inquiry on which they have been engaged forms only one branch of the general question of local taxation, and that other considerations, besides those which have been submitted to their investigation, should be previously taken into account in any general measure giving effect to the above recommendations.

APPENDIX IX.

TABLE A.—*Local Rates in England*, 1868.

[000's omitted from Cols. 1, 2, 3, and 4.]

	1	2	3	4	5	6	7	8
					Rates in £ on Rateable Value.			
England (1868).	Poor's Rate.	County, Borough, Police Rates, &c.	Improvement, District, Sewers, Drainage Rates, &c.	Total of all Rates (Cols. 1, 2, and 3).	Poor's Rate (Col. 1).	County Rates, &c. (Col. 2).	Improvement Rates, &c. (Col. 3).	All Rates.
	£	£	£	£	*s. d.*	*s. d.*	*s. d.*	*s. d.*
Bedford	60,	35,	12,	108,	1 11¾	1 1½	– 5	3 6
Berks	100,	54,	19,	173,	1 11¼	1 –¾	– 4½	3 4½
Bucks	99,	49,	4,	151,	2 1	1 –½	– 1	3 2½
Cambridge	89,	56,	57,	201,	1 8¼	1 –½	1 –¾	3 9½
Chester	154,	100,	95,	349,	1 3	– 10	– 9¼	2 10¼
Cornwall	104,	70,	11,	185,	1 9½	1 2¾	– 2	3 2¼
Cumberland	58,	33,	22,	112,	1 1	– 7¼	– 4¾	2 1
Derby	92,	64,	19,	175,	1 2¾	– 10	– 3¼	2 4
Devon	217,	119,	66,	402,	1 8¾	– 11½	– 6½	3 2¾
Dorset	92,	52,	10,	154,	2 –	1 1½	– 3	3 4½
Durham	138,	77,	84,	299,	1 3	– 8¼	– 9	2 8¼
Essex	231,	101,	49,	381,	2 1¼	– 10¾	– 5¼	3 5¼
Gloucester	185,	111,	103,	398,	1 6¾	– 11	– 10¼	3 4
Hereford	56,	41,	8,	106,	1 4¼	1 –¼	– 2¼	2 6¾
Hertford	86,	51,	9,	145,	1 9¾	1 1	– 2¼	3 1
Huntingdon	29,	21,	39,	89,	1 4¼	– 11¾	1 10	4 2
Kent	304,	227,	180,	711,	1 7¼	1 2¼	– 11¼	3 8¾
Lancaster	736,	753,	339,	1,828,	1 4½	1 4¾	– 7¾	*3 5
Leicester	95,	57,	22,	174,	1 5¼	– 10¼	– 4	2 7½
Lincoln	171,	168,	91,	431,	1 2½	1 2¼	– 7½	3 –¼
Middlesex	1,105,	636,	1,116,	2,857,	1 6½	– 10¾	1 6½	3 11¾
Monmouth	73,	35,	12,	120,	2 2	1 –¼	– 4¼	3 6½
Norfolk	233,	76,	45,	354,	2 –	– 8¼	– 4¾	3 1
Northampton	113,	74,	15,	202,	1 8¼	1 1	– 2½	2 11¾
Northumberland	121,	106,	23,	250,	1 3½	1 2	– 3¼	2 8¾
Nottingham	89,	87,	36,	212,	1 3½	1 3¼	– 6	3 –¾
Oxford	84,	49,	15,	148,	1 8¾	1 –½	– 3¾	3 1
Rutland	11,	8,	—	20,	1 3¾	1 –¾	—	2 4½
Salop	76,	49,	18,	143,	1 –¾	– 8¼	– 3¼	2 –¼
Somerset	208,	110,	33,	351,	1 7¾	– 10¾	– 3	2 9½
Southampton	225,	82,	86,	393,	2 2¾	– 9½	– 10¼	3 10½
Stafford	190,	99,	99,	388,	1 3½	– 8¼	– 8¼	2 8
Suffolk	149,	76,	21,	246,	1 9¼	– 11	– 3	2 11¼
Surrey	420,	224,	383,	1,027,	1 9¾	– 11¾	1 8	4 5½
Sussex	206,	112,	83,	402,	2 –¾	1 1½	– 9¾	4 –
Warwick	167,	201,	38,	406,	1 3½	1 6¾	– 3½	3 1¾
Westmoreland	17,	11,	2,	31,	– 10	– 6¾	– 1½	1 6¼
Wilts	138,	73,	13,	224,	1 11½	1 –½	– 2¼	3 2¼
Worcester	95,	69,	35,	198,	1 3½	– 11¼	– 5¾	2 8½
York, East Riding	80,	88,	53,	221,	– 11½	1 –¾	– 7½	2 7¾
„ North „	87,	67,	35,	190,	1 1	– 9¾	– 5¼	2 4
„ West „	392,	344,	334,	1,069,	1 3¾	1 2¼	1 1¾	3 7¾
	7,375,	4,915,	3,734,	16,024,	†1 2¾	†1 1	†– 10¾	†3 2½
Avge. of all Engld.	—	—	—	—	1*s.* 6½*d.*	1*s.* –¼*d.*	9¼*d.*	3*s.* 4*d.*

* See note in Table C.

† Average for the three Ridings taken together.

TABLE B.—*Local Rates in England*, 1868, *Divided according to Districts.*

[000's omitted from Cols. 1, 2, 3, 4, and 5.]

Districts.	1 Poor's Rate.	2 County, Borough, Police Rates, &c.	3 Improvement, District, Sewers, Drainage Rates, &c.	4 Total of all Rates (Cols. 1, 2, and 3.	5 Rateable Value.	6 Rate in £ on Rateable Value. Poor's Rate (Col. 1).	7 County Rates, &c. (Col. 2).	8 Improvement Rates, &c. (Col. 3).	9 The Total of all Rates (Col. 4).
I. METROPOLIS.	£	£	£	£	£	s. d.	s. d.	s. d.	s. d.
Middlesex (including London and Westminster)	1,105,	636,	1,116,	2,857,	14,326,	1 6½	– 10½	1 6¾	3 11¾
II. SOUTH-EASTERN.									
Surrey	420,	224,	383,	1,027,	4,615,				
Kent	304,	227,	180,	711,	3,818,				
Sussex	206,	112,	83,	401,	1,999,				
Hants	225,	82,	87,	393,	2,035,				
Berks	100,	54,	19,	173,	1,020,				
	1,255,	699,	752,	2,705,	13,488,	1 10¼	1 –½	1 1¼	4 –
III. S. MIDLAND.									
Herts	86,	51,	9,	145,	940,				
Bucks	99,	49,	4,	152,	949,				
Oxon	84,	49,	15,	148,	957,				
Northampton	113,	73,	15,	202,	1,355,				
Hunts	29,	21,	39,	89,	425,				
Beds	60,	35,	13,	108,	612,				
Cambridge	89,	56,	56,	201,	1,064,				
	560,	334,	151,	1,045,	6,302,	1 9¼	1 –¾	– 5¾	3 3¾
IV. EASTERN.									
Essex	231,	101,	49,	381,	2,227,				
Suffolk	149,	76,	21,	246,	1,663,				
Norfolk	233,	76,	45,	354,	2,294,				
	613,	253,	115,	981,	6,184,	1 11¾	– 9¾	– 4½	3 2
V. SOUTH-WESTERN.									
Wilts	138,	73,	13,	224,	1,405,				
Dorset	92,	52,	10,	154,	915,				
Devon	217,	119,	66,	402,	2,482,				
Cornwall	104,	70,	11,	185,	1,150,				
Somerset	208,	110,	33,	351,	2,534,				
	759,	424,	133,	1,316,	8,486,	1 9¼	1 –	– 3¾	3 1
VI. W. MIDLAND.									
Gloucester	185,	111,	103,	398,	2,384,				
Hereford	56,	41,	8,	100,	827,				
Salop	76,	49,	18,	143,	1,418,				
Stafford	190,	99,	99,	388,	2,921,				
Worcester	95,	69,	35,	198,	1,472,				
Warwick	167,	201,	37,	406,	2,577,				
	769,	570,	300,	1,630,	11,599	1 3¾	– 11¾	– 6¼	2 9¾

TABLE B.—*Local Rates in England*, 1868—*Contd.*

[000's omitted from Cols. 1, 2, 3, 4, and 5.]

Districts.	1 Poor's Rate.	2 County, Borough, Police Rates, &c.	3 Improvement, District, Sewers, Drainage Rates, &c.	4 Total of all Rates (Cols. 1, 2, and 3).	5 Rateable Value.	6 Rate in £ on Rateable Value. Poor's Rate (Col. 1).	7 County Rates, &c. (Col. 2).	8 Improvement Rates, &c. (Col. 3).	9 The Total of all Rates (Col. 4).
VII. N. MIDLAND.	£	£	£	£	£	*s. d.*	*s. d.*	*s. d.*	*s. d.*
Leicester	95,	57,	22,	174,	1,322,				
Rutland	11,	8,	—	19,	160,				
Lincoln	171,	168,	91,	431,	2,851,				
Notts	89,	87,	36,	212,	1,381,				
Derby	92,	64,	19,	175,	1,505,				
	458,	384,	168,	1,011,	7,219,	1 3¼	1 -¾	- 5½	2 9½
VIII. N.-WESTERN.									
Cheshire	154,	100,	95,	349,	2,486,				
Lancaster	736,	753,	339,	1,828,	10,721,				
	890,	853,	434,	2,177,	13,207,	1 4	1 3¼	- 8	3 3¼
IX. YORK.									
North Riding	87,	67,	35,	190,	1,622,				
East "	80,	88,	53,	221,	1,671,				
West "	392,	344,	334,	1,069,	5,903,				
	559,	499,	422,	1,480,	9,196,	1 2¾	1 1	- 1	3 2¾
X. NORTHERN.									
Durham	138,	77,	84,	299,	2,220,				
Northumberland	121,	106,	22,	249,	1,832,				
Cumberland	58,	33,	22,	112,	1,069,				
Westmoreland	16,	11,	3,	31,	403,				
	333,	227,	131,	691,	5,524,	1 2½	- 9¾	- 5¾	2 6

TABLE B *contd.—Poor's Rate as in Table above, and as Levied on an Income Tax Assessment.*

Name of Division.	Rate in £. Poor's Rate as in Table above.	Maximum Rate = 100. — Proportions thereof.	Name of Division.	Rate in £ of Poor's Rate on Income Tax Assessment.	Maximum Rate = 100. — Proportions thereof.
	s. d.			*s. d.*	
Eastern	1 11¾	100	Eastern	– 9¼	100
South-Eastern	1 10¼	94	South-Eastern	– 8½	92
South Midland	1 9¼	90	South Midland	– 8¼	89
South-Western	1 9¼	90	South-Western	– 7¾	84
North-Western	1 4	67	West Midland	– 6¼	68
West Midland	1 3¾	66	Northern	– 5½	59
North Midland	1 3¼	64	North Midland	– 5¼	57
York	1 2¾	62	North-Western	– 5	54
Northern	1 2½	61	York	– 4½	49

BLE C.—*Incidence of* ALL *Rates for Counties in England for* 1868, *after Deducting Towns Represented in Parliament* (*Cols.* 1 *and* 2), *the same on Aggregate for Towns Represented* (*Cols.* 3, 4, *and* 5), *and also on the Counties, including Towns Represented* (*Cols.* 6, 7, *and* 8).

Counties of England (Middlesex and Surrey excluded).	1 Rate in £ of all Rates, Deducting Towns Represented.	2 Maximum Rate = 100. —— Proportions thereof.	3 Counties of England (Middlesex, Surrey, and Rutland excluded).	4 Rate in £ of all Rates on Towns Represented.	5 Maximum Rate = 100. —— Proportions thereof.	6 Counties of England (Middlesex and Surrey excluded).	7 Rate in £ of all Rates.	8 Maximum Rate = 100. —— Proportions thereof.
	s. d.			*s. d.*			*s. d.*	
luntingdon	4 4	100	Norfolk	5 6¼	100	Hunts	4 2¼	100
ssex	3 11¼	90	Bedford	5 4	97	Sussex	4 -¼	96
mbridge	3 8½	85	Kent	5 1¾	94	Southampton	3 10½	92
ancaster*	3 8	85	Devon	4 10¾	89	Cambridge	3 9¼	90
Ionmouth	3 5	79	York, West	4 10¾	89	Kent	3 8¾	90
ledford	3 4¼	77	Southamptn.	4 10¼	88	York, West	3 7½	86
outhampton	3 4¼	77	Essex	4 9¼	87	Bedford	3 6½	84
ssex	3 4	77	Hertford	4 8½	85	Monmouth	3 6½	84
ornwall	3 3	75	Nottingham	4 8¼	85	Essex	3 5	82
orset	3 2¾	75	Leicester	4 4½	79	Lancaster	3 5*	82
erks	3 1¾	73	Chester	4 4	79	Berks	3 4¾	82
Vales	3 1¾	73	Cambridge	4 3¼	77	Dorset	3 4½	80
ent	3 1½	71	Berks	4 2¾	77	Gloucester	3 4	80
uckingham	3 1	71	Northmbrlnd	4 2½	76	Devon	3 2¾	78
Ixford	3 1	71	Suffolk	4 2¼	76	Cornwall	3 2¾	78
Wilts	3 1	71	Gloucester	4 1¾	76	Bucks	3 2½	76
Hertford	3 -½	69	Northamptn.	4 1½	74	Wilts	3 2¼	76
incoln	2 11¼	67	Wales	4 1½	74	Warwick	3 1¾	76
ork, West	2 10¼	65	Hereford	4 1	74	Herts	3 1	74
orthampton	2 9¾	65	Stafford	4 1	74	Norfolk	3 1	74
evon	2 9¼	64	Sussex	4 1	74	Oxford	3 1	74
ffolk	2 8¾	64	Warwick	4 1	74	Nottingham	3 -¾	74
merset	2 8¼	62	Durham	4 -½	73	Lincoln	3 -¼	72
rfolk	2 8¼	62	Monmouth	3 11¾	73	Northamptn.	2 11¾	72
ereford	2 4½	54	York, North	3 10½	70	Suffolk	2 11½	72
itland	2 4¼	54	Worcester	3 9¾	70	Chester	2 9¾	68
hester	2 3½	52	Dorset	3 9½	68	Somerset	2 9¼	66
Varwick	2 3½	52	York, East	3 9¼	68	Northmbrlnd	2 8¾	66
Vorcester	2 3¼	52	Lincoln	3 8½	67	Worcester	2 8½	64
ork, East	2 3¼	52	Bucks	3 6¼	64	Durham	2 8¼	64
eicester	2 3	52	Derby	3 6	64	Stafford	2 8	64
urham	2 2¾	52	Wilts	3 4¼	61	York, East	2 7¾	64
ottingham	2 2¾	52	Cumberland	3 3¾	61	Leicester	2 7½	62
erby	2 2¼	50	Lancaster*	3 3	59	Hereford	2 6¾	62
loucester	2 1¾	50	Oxford	3 1½	56	Rutland	2 4½	56
tafford	2 -¼	46						
orthmbrlnd.	1 11½	44	Somerset	3 1½	56	Derby	2 4	56
ork, North	1 10¾	44	Cornwall	3 -½	56	York, North	2 4	56
alop	1 10	42	Salop	2 10½	52	Cumberland	2 1	50
umberland	1 9¾	42	Westmorlnd.	2 4	42	Salop	2 -¾	50
Vestmorelnd.	1 5	33	Huntingdon	2 3	41	Westmorlnd.	1 6¼	36

* The special Liverpool rates are not included in this return.

TABLE C *contd.—Incidence of County, Hundred, Borough, Police, Highway, Chur Lighting and Watching Rates (Col. 1), and of Improvement, General District, Comm sioners of Sewers, Drainage and Embankment Rates (Col. 2), for Counties in Englan*

County.	1 Rate in £ of County, Borough, Police, &c., Rates.	Maximum Rate = 100. Proportions thereof.	County.	2 Rate in £ of Improvement, District, &c., Rates.	Maximum Rate = 100 Proportions thereof.
	s. *d.*			*s.* *d.*	
Warwick	1 6¾	100	Huntingdon	1 10	100
Lancaster	1 4¾	89	Surrey	1 8	91
Nottingham	1 3¼	81	Middlesex	1 6½	84
Cornwall	1 2¾	79	Cambridge	1 –¾	58
Kent	1 2¼	76	Kent	– 11¼	51
Lincoln	1 2¼	76	York	– 10¾	49
Northumberland	1 2	75	Gloucester	– 10½	47
Bedford	1 1½	72	Southampton	– 10¼	47
Dorset	1 1½	72	Sussex	– 9¾	44
Sussex	1 1½	72	Chester	– 9¼	42
Hertford	1 1	69	Durham	– 9	41
Northampton	1 1	69	Stafford	– 8¼	38
York	1 1	69	Lancaster	– 7¾	35
Berks	1 –¾	68	Lincoln	– 7½	34
Rutland	1 –¾	68	Devon	– 6½	30
Bucks	1 –½	67	Nottingham	– 6	27
Cambridge	1 –½	67	Worcester	– 5¾	26
Oxford	1 –½	67	Essex	– 5¼	24
Wilts	1 –½	67	Bedford	– 5	23
Hereford	1 –¼	65	Cumberland	– 4¾	22
Monmouth	1 –¼	65	Norfolk	– 4¾	22
Huntingdon	– 11¾	63	Berks	– 4½	20
Surrey	– 11¾	63	Monmouth	– 4¼	19
Devon	– 11½	61	Leicester	– 4	18
Worcester	– 11¼	60	Oxford	– 3¾	17
Gloucester	– 11	59	Warwick	– 3½	16
Suffolk	– 11	59	Derby	– 3¼	15
Essex	– 10¾	57	Northumberland	– 3¼	15
Middlesex	– 10¾	57	Salop	– 3¼	15
Somerset	– 10¾	57	Dorset	– 3	14
Leicester	– 10¼	55	Somerset	– 3	14
Chester	– 10	53	Suffolk	– 3	14
Derby	– 10	53	Northampton	– 2½	11
Southampton	– 9½	51	Hereford	– 2¼	10
Durham	– 8¼	44	Hertford	– 2¼	10
Norfolk	– 8¼	44	Wilts	– 2¼	10
Salop	– 8¼	44	Cornwall	– 2	9
Stafford	– 8¼	44	Westmoreland	– 1½	7 nea
Cumberland	– 7¼	37	Bucks	– 1	5 nea
Westmoreland	– 6¾	36			

Table D.—*Ratio of Poor's Rate* (1868) *to Population* (1861), *for Counties in England.*

County.	Rate per Head of Poor's Rates (1868) to Population of 1861.	Maximum Rate = 100. — Proportions thereof.	County.	Rate per Head of Poor's Rates (1868) to Population of 1861.	Maximum Rate = 100. — Proportions thereof.	County.	Rate per Head of Poor's Rates (1868) to Population of 1861.	Maximum Rate = 100. — Proportions thereof.
	s. d.			s. d.			s. d.	
Bucks	11 9	100	Southmptn.	9 4	79	Cardigan	7 –½	60 nearly
Essex	11 5	97	Carnarvon	9 2¾	79			
Sussex	11 4	96	Hereford	9 1¼	77	Nrthumbrlnd	7 –½	60
Berks	11 3¾	96	Hntngdn.	9 1 nearly	77	Brecknock	6 5½	55
Wilts	11 1½	94				Salop	6 3½	53
Norfolk	10 9	91	Bedford	8 11¼	76	Nottingham	6 2	53
Anglesey	10 8¾	91	Montgomry.	8 10½	75	Worcester	6 2	53
Cambridge	10 1½	86	Suffolk	8 10	75	Chester	6 –¾	52
Surrey	10 1	86	Monmouth	8 4½	71	Lancaster	6 –¾	52
Merioneth	10 –	85	Kent	8 4	71	Warwick	5 11½	51
Middlesex	10 –	85	Lincoln	8 3¾	71	York, E., including city	5 8¼	48
Nrthamptn.	9 11½	84	Glamorgan	8 –¾	69			
Hertford	9 10¾	84	Leicester	7 11¾	68	Cornwall	5 7½	48
Dorset	9 9¾	83	Pembroke....	7 11¾	68	Cumberland	5 7½	48
Flint	9 9¼	83	Denbigh	7 9	66	Durham	5 6½	47
Oxford........	9 9¼	83	Gloucester	7 7	65	Westmorlnd.	5 6½	47
Rutland	9 7½	81	Carmarthen	7 5½	63	Derby	5 5¼	46
Radnor	9 4¾	80	Devon	7 5	63	York, West	5 2¼	44
Somerset	9 4	79	York, North	7 1½	60	Stafford	5 1	43

Table E.—*Incidence of Property and Income Tax Levied on Rateable Value for Counties named.*

[000's omitted from Columns of Property and Income Tax.]

England. — Counties (including Boroughs), Middlesex and Surrey omitted.	Property and Income Tax, Year ending 5th April, 1863, under Schedules A, B, D, and E.	Rate in the £ of the Property and Income Tax on the Rateable Value, 1868.	England. — Counties (including Boroughs).	Property and Income Tax, Year ending 5th April, 1863, under Schedules A, B, D, and E.	Rate in the £ of the Property and Income Tax on the Rateable Value, 1868.
	£	s. d.		£	s. d.
Bedford	37,	1 2½	Monmouth	44,	1 3¼
Berks	65,	1 3¼	Norfolk	148,	1 3¼
Bucks	54,	1 1¾	Northampton	82,	1 2¾
Cambridge	71,	1 3¾	Northumberland	122,	1 3¾
Chester	156,	1 3¼	Nottingham	90,	1 3½
Cornwall	74,	1 3¼	Oxford	64,	1 3¾
Cumberland	58,	1 –¾	Rutland..................	10,	1 3¼
Derby	133,	1 9	Salop	88,	1 3
Devon	153,	1 2¾	Somerset	145,	1 1¼
Dorset	57,	1 3¼	Southampton	131,	1 3¼
Durham	142,	1 3¼	Stafford	205,	1 4¾
Essex	132,	1 2¼	Suffolk	103,	1 3
Gloucester	193,	1 7½	Sussex	127,	1 3¼
Hereford	44,	1 –¾	Warwick	203,	1 7
Hertford	59,	1 3¼	Westmoreland	19,	– 11¼
Huntingdon	25,	1 2¼	Wilts	89,	1 3¼
Kent	224,	1 2¼	Worcester	94,	1 3¼
Lancaster	1,063,	1 11¾	York, East	101,	1 2¾
Leicester	80,	1 2½	,, North	147,	1 9½
Lincoln	176,	1 2¾	,, West	439,	1 5¾

Note.—This table is framed from Return 283/259 of 1864, House of Commons.

TABLE F.—*Incidence of Poor's Rate on Assessment to Property and Income Tax for Counties named.*

County.	Rate in the £ of Poor's Rate, 1868, on Assessment for Income and Property Tax for Schedules A, B, and D, 1869-70.		Maximum Rate = 100. — Proportions thereof.	County.	Rate in the £ of Poor's Rate, 1868, on Rateable Value.		Maximum Rate = 100. — Proportions thereto.
	s.	*d.*			*s.*	*d.*	
Gloucester	–	10½	100	Southampton	2	2¾	100
Monmouth	–	10½	100	Monmouth	2	2	97
Bucks	–	10¼	98	Essex	2	1¼	94
Essex	–	10¼	98	Bucks	2	1	93
Southampton	–	10¼	98	Sussex	2	–¾	92
Dorset	–	9½	90	Dorset	2	–	90
Berks	–	9¼	88	Norfolk	2	–	90
Norfolk	–	9¼	88	Bedford	1	11¾	89
Sussex	–	9¼	88	Wilts	1	11½	88
Wilts	–	9	86	Berks	1	11¼	87
Bedford	–	8¾	83	Hertford	1	9¾	81
Cornwall	–	8½	81	Surrey	1	9¾	81
Devon	–	8¼	79	Cornwall	1	9½	80
Northampton	–	8¼	79	Suffolk	1	9¼	80
Suffolk	–	8¼	79	Devon	1	8¾	77
Oxford	–	8	76	Oxford	1	8¾	77
Kent	–	7¾	74	Cambridge	1	8¼	76
Surrey	–	7½	71	Northampton	1	8¼	76
Hereford	–	7¼	69	Somerset	1	7¾	74
Cambridge	–	7	67	Kent	1	7¼	72
Huntingdon	–	7	67	Gloucester	1	6¾	70
Chester	–	6¾	64	Middlesex	1	6½	69
Leicester	–	6½	62	Leicester	1	5¼	64
Somerset	–	6¼	60	Lancaster	1	4½	62
Durham	–	6	57	Hereford	1	4¼	61
Northumberland	–	5¾	55	Huntingdon	1	4¼	61
Worcester	–	5¾	55	Rutland	1	3¾	59
Hertford	–	5½	52	Northumberland	1	3½	58
Lincoln	–	5½	52	Nottingham	1	3½	58
Nottingham	–	5½	52	Stafford	1	3½	58
Salop	–	5½	52	Warwick	1	3½	58
Stafford	–	5½	52	Worcester	1	3½	58
Westmoreland	–	5¼	50	Durham	1	3	56
Cumberland	–	5¼	50	Chester	1	3	56
Lancaster	–	4¾	45	Derby	1	2¾	55
Rutland	–	4¾	45	York	1	2¾	55
Warwick	–	4¾	45	Lincoln	1	2½	54
York	–	4¼	40	Cumberland	1	1	49
Derby	–	3¾	36	Salop	1	–¾	48
Middlesex	–	3½	33	Westmoreland	–	10	37

TABLE G.—*Incidence of Property and Income Tax Levied on Rateable Value for Counties named, after Deducting Towns Represented in Parliament.*

	1			2	
Counties.	Ratio of Property and Income Tax, Year ending 5th April, 1863, under Schedules A, B, D, and E, on Rateable Value for Counties named after Deducting Respective Proportions for Towns Represented in Parliament.		Counties.	Amounts in Column 1 Arranged in Proportional Order.	
	s.	*d.*		*s.*	*d.*
Bedford	1	1¾	Derby	1	9½
Berks	1	2¼	Lancaster	1	3¾
Bucks	1	1¾	Stafford	1	3¾
Cambridge	1	2¾	Durham	1	3¼
Chester	1	1¼	Rutland	1	3¼
Cornwall	1	3	Cornwall	1	3
Cumberland	-	11	Hertford	1	3
Derby	1	9½	Monmouth	1	3
Devon	1	-	Cambridge	1	2¾
Dorset	1	2¾	Dorset	1	2¾
Durham	1	3¼	Gloucester	1	2½
Essex	1	2	Berks	1	2¼
Gloucester	1	2½	Southampton	1	2¼
Hereford	1	-¼	Suffolk	1	2¼
Hertford	1	3	York, West	1	2¼
Huntingdon	1	1¾	Essex	1	2
Kent	1	1½	Oxford	1	2
Lancaster	1	3¾	Salop	1	2
Leicester	1	1½	Bedford	1	1¾
Lincoln	1	1¾	Bucks	1	1¾
Monmouth	1	3	Huntingdon	1	1¾
Norfolk	1	1¾	Lincoln	1	1¾
Northampton	1	1¾	Norfolk	1	1¾
Northumberland	1	-¼	Northampton	1	1¾
Nottingham	-	11	Wilts	1	1¾
Oxford	1	2	Kent	1	1½
Rutland	1	3¼	Leicester	1	1½
Salop	1	2	Chester	1	1¼
Somerset	1	1	Warwick	1	1¼
Southampton	1	2¼	Somerset	1	1
Stafford	1	3¾	Worcester	1	1
Suffolk	1	2¼	York, North	1	1
Sussex	1	-¼	Hereford	1	-¼
Warwick	1	1¼	Northumberland	1	-¼
Westmoreland	-	9¾	Sussex	1	-¼
Wilts	1	1¾	Devon	1	-
Worcester	1	1	York, East	-	11½
York, East	-	11½	Cumberland	-	11
„ North	1	1	Nottingham	-	11
„ West	1	2¼	Westmoreland	-	9¾

TABLE H.—*Incidence of* ALL *Rates on Places Represented in Parliament in England,* 1868.

Name of Place and County.	Rate in the £ on each Place Named.		Name of Place and County.	Rate in the £ on each Place Named.	
	s.	*d.*		*s.*	*d.*
Bedfordshire—			*Devonshire—*		
Bedford	5	4	Ashburton	2	6¾
			Barnstaple	3	11¼
			Dartmouth	2	6½
			Devonport	5	6
Berkshire—			Exeter (city)	4	2¼
Abingdon	4	8¾	Honiton	3	5½
Reading	4	9½	Plymouth	6	10
Wallingford	3	5½	Tavistock	2	8¼
Windsor	3	4	Tiverton	2	9¼
			Totnes	2	8¼
Buckingham—					
Aylesbury	3	4¾	*Dorsetshire—*		
Buckingham	3	5¾	Bridport	4	3
Chipping Wycombe	3	7¼	Dorchester	4	9½
Great Marlow	4	2¼	Lyme Regis	3	9
			Poole	5	7¾
			Shaftesbury	3	5
			Wareham	2	2
Cambridgeshire—			Weymouth and Mel-	3	11½
Cambridge	4	3¼	combe Regis }		
Chester—			*Durham—*		
Birkenhead	4	10¼	Durham (city)	2	3¼
Chester (city)	5	1	Gateshead	4	10
Macclesfield	3	8	South Shields	2	10
Stockport	3	3	Sunderland	4	5½
Cornwall—			*Essex—*		
Bodmin	2	6¾	Colchester	5	5
Helston	4	–	Harwich	3	8¼
Launceston	3	2¾	Maldon	3	4¼
Liskeard	3	1½			
Penrhyn and Falmouth	3	10¾			
St. Ives	2	7¼			
Truro	2	3¾	*Gloucester—*		
			Bristol (city)	4	3¼
			Cheltenham	4	–¾
			Cirencester	3	7¼
Cumberland—			Gloucester (city)	4	–¼
Carlisle (city)	3	1¾	Stroud	3	9½
Cockermouth	2	5	Tewkesbury	4	2½
Whitehaven	4	1¼			
			Hants—		
Derbyshire—			Andover	3	10½
Derby	3	6	Christchurch	2	1¾

TABLE H.—*Incidence of* ALL *Rates on Places Represented—Contd.*

Name of Place and County.	Rate in the £ on each Place Named.		Name of Place and County.	Rate in the £ on each Place Named.	
	s.	*d.*		*s.*	*d.*
Hants—contd.			*Lincoln—*		
Lymington	3	10¼	Boston	4	3½
Newport, Isle of Wight	2	3¾	Grantham	3	3½
			Gt. Grimsby	3	11
Petersfield	3	3	Lincoln (city).............	3	4
Portsmouth...............	6	9	Stamford....................	3	9½
Southampton	5	9½			
Winchester (city)	3	8¾			
			Monmouth—		
			Monmouth	4	4½
Hereford—			Newport-on-Usk...........	3	11½
Hereford (city)	4	7½	Usk	3	6¾
Leominster	3	1			
			Norfolk—		
Hertford—			Great Yarmouth	7	–
Hertford	4	8½	Kings Lynn	7	10¼
			Norwich (city)	4	7¾
Huntingdon—			Thetford	3	1¾
Huntingdon	2	3			
			Northampton—		
Kent—			Northampton	5	1
Canterbury................	4	7¾	Peterborough	2	4¼
Chatham	3	3¼			
Dover	5	11¼			
Greenwich	5	7¾	*Northumberland—*		
Hythe	3	1¾	Berwick-on-Tweed........	2	6¼
Maidstone	6	2½	Morpeth	1	10
Rochester..................	4	2¾	Newcastle-on-Tyne	4	11
Sandwich	4	5½	Tynemouth and North Shields........	3	7½
Lancaster—					
Ashton-under-Lyne	3	1			
Blackburn	1	11½	*Nottingham—*		
Bolton	4	2¾	East Retford	3	2¼
Bury	2	10¾	Newark	4	11¼
Clitheroe..................	2	1¾	Nottingham	5	7½
Lancaster	2	10			
Liverpool..................	2	1½			
Manchester (city)	4	–½	*Oxford—*		
Oldham	4	3½	Banbury	4	1½
Preston	5	8¼	Oxford.....................	3	2¼
Rochdale..................	3	3¼	Woodstock	2	2½
Salford....................	5	2			
Warrington	4	9¼			
Wigan	6	1			
Leicester—			*Salop—*		
Leicester..................	4	4½	Bridgnorth	2	8¾

TABLE H.—*Incidence of* ALL *Rates on Places Represented—Contd.*

Name of Place and County.	Rate in the £ on each Place Named.		Name of Place and County.	Rate in the £ on each Place Named.	
	s.	d.		s.	d.
Salop—contd.			*Westmoreland—*		
Ludlow	2	11	Kendal	2	4
Shrewsbury	3	3½			
Wenlock	2	2¼			
			Wilts—		
			Calne	3	5¾
Somerset—			Chippenham	3	5¾
Bath	3	5¼	Cricklade	2	8¼
Bridgwater	2	-½	Devizes	4	1½
Frome	2	11¼	Malmsbury	2	8¼
Taunton	2	8½	Salisbury	6	10¼
Wells	2	10	Westbury	3	1½
			Wilton	3	9¼
			Marlborough	4	-
Stafford—					
Lichfield	2	-¾			
Newcastle-under-Lyne	2	1¼	*Worcester—*		
Stafford	2	8¾	Bewdley	3	6¾
Stoke-on-Trent	4	11½	Droitwich	2	4½
Tamworth	1	10¾	Dudley	3	6¼
Walsall	3	1	Evesham	4	1¼
Wolverhampton	4	7	Kidderminster	4	4½
			Worcester	4	6
Suffolk—					
Bury St. Edmunds	5	-¼			
Eye	3	1¾	*York, North Riding—*		
Ipswich	4	7¾	Malton	3	4¾
			North Allerton	2	-
			Richmond	1	11
Surrey—			Scarborough	4	6¼
Guildford	5	-¼	Thirsk	1	7½
Reigate	3	10¼	Whitby	4	5¾
			York	4	6½
Sussex—			*York, East Riding—*		
Arundel	5	11¾	Beverley	3	5½
Brighton	5	6¼	Kingston-on-Hull	3	9½
Chichester	4	2½			
Hastings	3	2			
Horsham	3	8	*York, West Riding—*		
Lewes	4	11¼	Bradford	4	11¾
Midhurst	4	3¼	Halifax	4	1½
New Shoreham	2	1¼	Huddersfield	4	7
Rye	4	-¼	Knaresborough	3	3
			Leeds	5	9½
			Pontefract	4	6½
Warwick—			Ripon	1	10
Birmingham	4	-	Sheffield	4	5
Coventry	4	11	Wakefield	4	1
Warwick	4	-¾			

Note.—Average of all places named, 3s. 11¾d.

TABLE I.—*Incidence of Poor's Rates on Places Represented in Parliament in England, 1868.*

Name of Place and County.	Rate in the £ of the Poor's Rate on the Rateable Value for each Place Named.		Name of Place and County.	Rate in the £ of the Poor's Rate on the Rateable Value for each Place Named.	
	s.	d.		s.	d.
Bedfordshire—			*Devonshire—Contd.*		
Bedford	1	9¾	Dartmouth	1	1
			Devonport	2	5½
Berks—			Exeter (city)	1	8¾
Abingdon	1	10¾	Honiton	2	2
Reading	1	11	Plymouth	3	6½
Wallingford	2	3¼	Tavistock	1	10¼
Windsor	1	8½	Lincoln	1	2¾
			Totnes	1	6¼
Buckingham—					
Aylesbury	2	3½	*Dorsetshire—*		
Buckingham	2	-¾	Bridport	2	1¾
Chipping Norton	2	7½	Dorchester	1	11½
Great Marlow	2	5¾	Lyme Regis	2	1½
			Poole	2	1½
Cambridgeshire—			Shaftesbury	1	10½
Cambridge	2	1½	Wareham	1	8¼
			Weymouth and Melcombe Regis	2	-¾
Chester—					
Birkenhead	1	8¾	*Durham—*		
Chester (city)	2	2½	Durham (city)	1	-
Macclesfield	1	7	Gateshead	1	8½
Stockport	1	-½	South Shields	1	8
			Sunderland	1	10¼
Cornwall—					
Bodmin	1	8	*Essex—*		
Helston	2	4	Colchester	3	2¾
Launceston	1	6	Harwich	1	9
Liskeard	1	10¾	Maldon	1	6¼
Penrhyn and Falmouth	1	11			
St. Ives	1	3½	*Gloucester—*		
Truro	1	5¾	Bristol (city)	1	9
			Cheltenham	1	8¾
			Cirencester	-	11½
Cumberland—			Gloucester (city)	1	-¾
Carlisle (city)	1	5	Stroud	2	5¾
Cockermouth	-	11½	Tewkesbury	1	8¼
Whitehaven	1	3¼			
			Hants—		
Derbyshire—			Andover	2	1¼
Derby	1	7½	Christ Church	1	1¼
			Lymington	2	10¼
Devonshire—			Newport, Isle of Wight	1	2
Ashburton	1	2½	Petersfield	2	2¼
Barnstaple	1	6½	Portsmouth	3	11¼

Table I.—*Incidence of Poor's Rates on Places Represented—Contd.*

Name of Place and County.	Rate in the £ of the Poor's Rate on the Rateable Value for each Place Named.		Name of Place and County.	Rate in the £ of the Poor's Rate on the Rateable Value for each Place Named.	
	s.	d.		s.	d.
Hants—Contd.			*Lincoln—*		
Southampton	2	9	Boston	2	1¼
Winchester (city)	2	1	Grantham	1	4¼
			Great Grimsby	—	11½
			Lincoln (city)	1	2¼
			Stamford	1	8
Hereford—					
Hereford (city)	1	1			
Leominster	1	2¼			
			Monmouth—		
			Monmouth	2	—¼
			Newport-on-Usk	2	—¼
Hertford—			Usk	2	1½
Hertford	2	6			
Huntingdon—			*Norfolk—*		
Huntingdon	1	5¾	Great Yarmouth	4	9
			King's Lynn	5	1¾
			Norwich (city)	3	1¾
Kent—			Thetford	1	8¾
Canterbury (city)	1	11¾			
Chatham	1	6¾			
Dover	1	11½			
Greenwich	2	—½	*Northampton—*		
Hythe	1	2¼	Northampton	1	11¼
Maidstone	2	5½	Peterborough	1	—
Rochester (city)	2	2¾			
Sandwich	1	9			
			Northumberland—		
			Berwick-on-Tweed	1	5½
Lancaster—			Morpeth	1	1½
Ashton-under-Lyne	1	2	Newcastle-on-Tyne	2	2¾
Blackburn	1	3	Tynemouth and North Shields	1	5
Bolton	1	6¼			
Bury	1	1½			
Clitheroe	—	9¾			
Lancaster	1	—½			
Liverpool	1	5½			
Manchester (city)	1	7¾	*Nottingham—*		
Oldham	1	7½	East Retford	1	6¼
Preston	1	8¼	Newark	1	1¾
Rochdale	1	5	Nottingham	1	9
Salford	1	10¾			
Warrington	1	6			
Wigan	—	6½			
			Oxford—		
			Banbury	1	9¼
Leicester—			Oxford	1	11¼
Leicester	2	2½	Woodstock	1	4¼

TABLE I.—*Incidence of Poor's Rate on Places Represented—Contd.*

Name of Place and County.	Rate in the £ of the Poor's Rate on the Rateable Value for each Place Named.	
	s.	*d.*
Salop—		
Bridgnorth	1	–¼
Ludlow	1	2¾
Shrewsbury	1	–
Wenlock	1	6¾
Somerset—		
Bath	1	2
Bridgwater	1	3¼
Frome	1	9¾
Taunton	1	6
Wells	1	6
Stafford—		
Lichfield (city)	–	9¼
Newcastle-under-Lyne	–	9
Stafford	1	–¾
Stoke-on-Trent	2	3½
Tamworth	1	3½
Walsall	1	7
Wolverhampton	1	11¾
Suffolk—		
Bury St. Edmunds	2	11
Eye	2	2¼
Ipswich	2	5¼
Surrey—		
Guildford	2	4¼
Reigate	1	5
Sussex—		
Arundel	4	2¼
Brighton	2	6
Chichester	2	6¾
Hastings	1	2
Horsham	3	1¾
Lewes	3	–¾
Midhurst	2	8¾
New Shoreham	–	9½
Rye	2	7¼
Warwick—		
Birmingham	1	5½
Coventry	1	11½
Warwick	1	4
Westmoreland—		
Kendal	–	9
Wilts—		
Calne	2	4
Chippenham	1	10¾
Cricklade	1	6¼
Devizes	1	10½
Malmsbury	1	9
Salisbury	2	8¾
Westbury	2	2¾
Wilton	2	3¼
Marlborough	2	3¼
Worcester—		
Bewdley	2	–¼
Droitwich	1	2¾
Dudley	1	1¾
Evesham	1	2½
Kidderminster	2	2¾
Worcester	1	10
York, North Riding—		
Malton	–	9¼
North Allerton	–	10¾
Richmond	1	3
Scarborough	–	11¾
Thirsk	–	9½
Whitby	2	3¾
York	–	10¼
York, East Riding—		
Beverley	–	8¾
Kingston-on-Hull	1	2¼
York, West Riding—		
Bradford	1	–¼
Halifax	1	3¼
Huddersfield	1	3¼
Knaresborough	–	7½
Leeds	1	11¼
Pontefract	2	1½
Ripon	–	11
Sheffield	1	10
Wakefield	1	5¾

Note.—Average of all places named, 1*s.* 8¾*d.*

TABLE K.—*Incidence of County, Hundred, Borough and Police, and of Highway, Distri Improvement, &c., Rates on Places Represented in Parliament in England*, 1868.

Name of Place and County.	Rates in the £ for each Place Named. County, Hundred, Borough, and Police Rates on the Rateable Value.		Rates in the £ for each Place Named. Highway, District, Improvement, Sewers Rates, &c.	
	s.	*d.*	*s.*	*d.*
Bedfordshire—				
Bedford	1	–½	2	5½
Berks—				
Abingdon	–	2½	2	9½
Reading	–	11½	1	11
Wallingford	–	6	–	8½
Windsor	1	3½	1	8¼
Buckingham—				
Aylesbury	–	5	–	8½
Buckingham	–	7½	–	8½
Chipping Wycombe	–	7¾	2	1¼
Great Marlow	–	5¼	1	1¾
Cambridgeshire—				
Cambridge	1	2¾	–	11
Chester—				
Birkenhead	–	3	3	1¾
Chester (city)	1	1¼	1	7¾
Macclesfield	–	8½	1	4
Stockport	–	10¼	1	7¼
Cornwall—				
Bodmin	–	4¾	–	5¾
Helston	–	6¼	1	1½
Launceston	–	7	–	11
Liskeard	–	4	–	10
Penrhyn and Falmouth	–	8¾	1	3
St. Ives	–	4¼	–	11½
Truro	–	2½	–	5
Cumberland—				
Carlisle (city)	–	2¼	1	6½
Cockermouth	–	4¼	1	7½
Whitehaven	–	7	2	2¾
Derbyshire—				
Derby	–	5	1	4¼
Devonshire—				
Ashburton	–	5	–	11¼
Barnstaple	1	–	1	4¾
Dartmouth	–	4½	7	6½
Devonport	–	11	2	6½
Exeter (city)	–	9¾	1	7½
Honiton	–	6½	–	8¾
Plymouth	1	–	2	3¼
Tavistock	–	3¼	–	6½
Tiverton	–	8¾	–	9
Totnes	–	5½	–	8½
Dorsetshire—				
Bridport	–	7¼	1	6¼
Dorchester	–	5¼	3	3
Lyme Regis	–	7¼	–	10¾
Poole	–	10¾	1	7¾
Shaftesbury	–	5¾	1	1
Wareham	–	3¼	–	2½
Weymouth and Melcombe Regis	–	7	–	3
Durham—				
Durham (city)	–	3¼	1	–
Gateshead	1	3½	1	9¾
South Shields	–	5¾	–	1¾
Sunderland	–	6½	2	2¼
Essex—				
Colchester	–	10¼	1	4¼
Harwich	–	–½	1	10
Maldon	–	10¼	–	9½
Gloucester—				
Bristol (city)	–	9¾	1	5½
Cheltenham	–	3¾	2	–¼
Cirencester	1	6	1	1¾
Gloucester (city)	–	5¾	2	4
Stroud	–	4¼	–	11½
Tewkesbury	–	4	2	2¼
Hants—				
Andover	–	6¾	1	3

[T]ABLE K.—*Incidence of County, Borough, &c., Rates on Places Represented in Parliament —Contd.*

Name of Place and County.	Rates in the £ for each Place Named. County, Hundred, Borough, and Police Rates on the Rateable Value.		Highway, District, Improvement, Sewers Rate, &c.	
	s.	d.	s.	d.
[H]ants—Contd.				
Christ Church	—		1	1¼
Lymington	–	5½	–	6½
Newport, Isle of Wight	–	4½	–	11¼
Petersfield	–	5	–	10¾
Portsmouth	–	8¼	2	4¼
Southampton	–	10	3	5¼
Winchester (city)	–	6¾	–	2¾
[H]ereford—				
Hereford (city)	2	–¾	1	11½
Leominster	–	6¾	–	10¼
[H]ertford—				
Hertford	–	9¼	1	5
[H]untingdon—				
Huntingdon	–	4	–	5¼
[K]ent—				
Canterbury (city)	–	9	1	5
Chatham	–	7½	1	1½
Dover	–	10¼	3	2½
Greenwich	–	7½	–	9½
Hythe	–	11	1	–¼
Maidstone	–	10½	1	10½
Rochester	–	8¾	1	3½
Sandwich	–	7½	–	3½
[La]ncaster—				
Ashton-under-Lyne	–	9¼	–	8
Blackburn	–	7½	–	1¼
Bolton	1	6	1	1¾
Bury	–	5	–	1
Clitheroe	–	4¾	–	8
Lancaster	–	2	3	6
Liverpool	–	4½	–	6¼
Manchester (city)	1	10	–	6½
Oldham	–	4¼	2	4
Preston	–	8¼	3	5
Rochdale	–	5½	–	7¾
Salford	1	4	1	11½
Warrington	–	10¾	2	4½
Wigan	–	10	4	8½
Leicester—				
Leicester	–	9¾	1	4¾
Lincoln—				
Boston	–	3¾	1	10½
Grantham	–	6	1	2
Great Grimsby	–	2¾	2	4
Lincoln (city)	—		2	3
Stamford	–	7¾	1	5¾
Monmouth—				
Monmouth	–	9	1	7
Newport-on-Usk	–	9¾	1	3¾
Usk	–	6¼	–	11¼
Norfolk—				
Great Yarmouth	—		2	2¾
King's Lynn	–	8¾	2	2½
Norwich (city)	1	–	2	11¼
Thetford	–	5	1	–½
Northampton—				
Northampton	1	4	1	9¾
Peterborough	–	4½	–	11¾
Northumberland—				
Berwick-on-Tweed	–	3¾	–	11
Morpeth	–	5	–	5¾
Newcastle-on-Tyne	–	2¾	2	6
Tynemouth and North Shields	–	9	1	3½
Nottingham—				
East Retford	–	4¼	–	8
Newark	1	6¾	2	2½
Nottingham	–	11¾	2	10¾
Oxford—				
Banbury	[illegible]	9	2	2½
Oxford	–	–¼	1	3¾
Woodstock	–	5¼	–	4¾

TABLE K.—*Incidence of County, Borough, &c., Rates on Places Represented in Parliame —Contd.*

Name of Place and County.	County, Hundred, Borough, and Police Rates, on the Rateable Value.		Highway, District, Improvement, Sewers Rate, &c.		Name of Place and County.	County, Hundred, Borough, and Police Rates, on the Rateable Value.		Highway District, Improvement, Sewers Rat &c.	
	s.	d.	s.	d.		s.	d.	s.	d.
Salop—					*Westmoreland—*				
Bridgnorth	–	3½	2	1½	Kendal	–	3¼	1	3¼
Ludlow	–	6¾	1	1¾					
Shrewsbury	–	5	1	10½	*Wilts—*				
Wenlock	–	2¼	–	5½	Calne	–	5	–	8¼
					Chippenham	–	4	1	3
Somerset—					Cricklade	–	4	–	8¼
Bath	–	9¼	1	5¾	Devizes	–	7¼	–	4¼
Bridgwater	–	5¼	–	4	Malmsbury	–	4¼	–	6¼
Frome	–	3¼	–	10	Salisbury	1	1¼	2	10¼
Taunton	–	2¼	1	1	Westbury	–	3¾	–	7
Wells	–	8½	1	2¾	Wilton	–	11¼	1	2¼
					Marlborough	–	3¼	1	4½
Stafford—									
Lichfield (city)	–	7½	–	8¾	*Worcester—*				
Newcastle - under - Lyne	1	1¼	–		Bewdley	–	5¼	–	7½
Stafford	–	4	1	4	Droitwich	–	5½	–	9
Stoke-on-Trent	–	7½	–	8	Dudley	1	–	1	9½
Tamworth	–	4	–	4½	Evesham	–	6½	–	3½
Walsall	–	6½	1	–¾	Kidderminster	1	1¼	1	–¾
Wolverhampton	–	10½	1	–¾	Worcester	–	11¼	1	9¼
Suffolk—					*York, North Riding—*				
Bury St. Edmunds	–	3¼	1	10	Malton	–	3	1	8¼
Eye	–	3¾	–	8¼	North Allerton	–	3½	–	9½
Ipswich	–	7¼	1	7¼	Richmond	–	2¾	–	5½
					Scarborough	–	8¼	2	9½
Surrey—					Thirsk	–	4	–	6½
Guildford	–	8½	1	4	Whitby	–	6	1	8
Reigate	–	7½	1	6½	York	2	4¼	1	4
Sussex—					*York, East Riding—*				
Arundel	–	3¾	1	5¾	Beverley	–	1½	2	5¼
Brighton	–	9¾	2	2½	Kingston-on-Hull	–	3¼	2	–¾
Chichester	1	4¼	–	4¾					
Hastings	–	5¼	1	7	*York, West Riding—*				
Horsham	–	6½	–		Bradford	–	7½	3	4
Lewes	–	9¼	–	9	Halifax	–	8½	2	4½
Midhurst	–	6¼	–	10	Huddersfield	–	4	2	9
New Shoreham	–	4¾	–	4	Knaresborough	–	9¾	–	10½
Rye	–	7½	–	7¾	Leeds	–	11¾	2	10½
					Pontefract	–	9	1	8
Warwick—					Ripon	–	10¾	–	
Birmingham	1	–½	1	6¼	Sheffield	–	4¼	2	3½
Coventry	–	9½	2	1¼	Wakefield	–	9¾	1	10¼
Warwick	–	7	2	2					

Note.—Average of all the places named   – 8¾ | 1 5?

TABLE L.—*Proportion per Head of Assessment under Schedule A to Population in the Counties of England named, for the Years* 1803 *and* 1867-68.

Name of County.	Proportion per Head of Assessment, Schedule A, 1803, to Population, 1801.			Name of County.	Proportion per Head of Assessment, Schedule A, 1867-68, to Population, 1861.		
	£	*s.*	*d.*		£	*s.*	*d.*
Lincolu	6	–	2	Lincoln	8	13	10¼
Northampton	5	3	11½	Northampton	6	17	10½
Bucks	4	14	9	Berks	6	13	11¼
Essex	4	8	10	Wilts	6	11	7
Berks	4	5	3¼	Essex	6	11	2
Wilts	4	4	8¾	Salop	6	10	–
Salop	4	4	2¼	Bucks	6	9	8
Bedford	4	3	4½	Hertford	6	8	7
Hertford	4	2	1	Norfolk	6	8	5¾
Chester	4	–	2¾	Surrey	6	6	10¾
Worcester	3	19	8	Kent	6	5	9¼
Norfolk	3	19	5¾	Suffolk	6	1	8¾
Surrey	3	19	2½	Bedford	5	14	5¼
Suffolk	3	14	–¾	Worcester	5	9	8¾
Gloucester	3	13	11	Warwick	5	8	8¼
York	3	12	6	York	5	6	5¼
Devon	3	11	9¼	Gloucester	5	4	8¾
Warwick	3	10	7½	Devon	5	4	6¼
Durham	3	10	6½	Chester	5	2	11½
Kent	3	9	7½	Lancaster	4	16	2½
Lancaster	2	16	2¾	Durham	3	12	9½

TABLE M.—*Account Showing the Increase in Property Assessed on each occasion of New Assessment from 1853 to 1867.   Schedule A, Great Britain.*

	Gross Annual Value Assessed in the Year.		Increase in 1857 over 1853.		
			Amount of Increase.	Increase per Cent.	
	1853.	1857.		In 4 Years.	Per Year.
	£	£	£		
Lands, tithes, manors, and fines .... }	47,559,474	49,572,873	2,013,339	4·23	1·06
Houses	46,959,338	52,142,449	5,183,161	11·03	2·76

	Gross Annual Value Assessed in the Year 1861.	Increase in 1861 over 1857.		
		Amount of Increase.	Increase per Cent.	
			In 4 Years.	Per Year.
	£	£		
Lands, tithes, manors, and fines .... }	51,752,772	2,179,899	4·39	1·10
Houses	58,590,395	6,447,896	12·36	3·09

	Gross Annual Value Assessed in the Year 1864.	Increase in 1864 over 1861.			Gross Annual Value Assessed in the Year 1867.
		Amount of Increase.	Increase per Cent.		
			In 4 Years.	Per Year.	
	£	£			£
Lands, tithes, manors, and fines .... }	53,605,984	1,898,212	3·66	1·22	55,280,861
Houses	65,087,088	6,496,693	11·09	3·69	74,588,966

	Increase in 1867 over 1864.			Increase in 1867 over 1853.		
	Amount of Increase.	Increase per Cent.		Amount of Increase.	Increase per Cent.	
		In 3 Years.	Per Year.		In 14 Years.	Per Year.
	£			£		
Lands, tithes, manors, and fines .... }	1,629,877	3·04	1·01	7,721,387	16·23	1·16
Houses	9,471,878	14·55	4·85	27,599,628	58·77	4·19

Note.—" Report of the Commissioners of Inland Revenue, 1870," vol. i, p. 129.

TABLE M *contd.—Annual Value of Various Descriptions of Real Property in England and Wales in Financial Year 1814-15, Compared with 1848.*

Schedule A of Property Tax. Description of Real Property Assessed.	Year 1814-15.		Year 1848-49.	
	Annual Value of Property Described.	Ratio Borne by each Description to the Total. Annual Value.	Annual Value of Property Described.	Ratio Borne by each Description to the Total. Annual Value.
	£	Per cnt.	£	Per cnt.
1. Lands	34,330,000	64·2	42,348,000	44·8
2. Messuages, including houses, shops, and warehouses	14,895,000	27·8	38,822,000	41·1
3. Sundries, including tithes	4,270,000	8·0	13,368,000	14·1
Total	53,495,000	100·0	94,538,000	100·0

Note.—From Statistical Society's *Journal,* vol. xx, p. 271 (Mr. F. Hendriks).

Amount and Ratio of Gross Assessment in 1864-65 of Lands and Other Real Property under Schedule A in England and Wales.

Description of Real Property Assessed.	Annual Value of Property Described.	Ratio Borne.
	£	Per cnt.
Lands including tithe rent charge	46,403,437	35·3
Other descriptions	84,938,062	64·7
Total	131,341,499	100·0

Note.—From Statistical Society's *Journal,* vol. xxxii, p. 314 (Mr. F. Purdy).

TABLE N.—*Amount of County Rate, &c., and of the Various Receipts in England and Wales, according to the Accounts of the County Treasurers for the Years stated below.*

[000's omitted.]

Receipts, Years ending Michaelmas.	County and Police Rates.	Allowance from Treasury.	Other Receipts.	Total.	Amount of Debt, &c.
ENGLAND.	£	£	£	£	£
1856	950,	236,	218,	1,593,	1,726,
'57	1,089,	210,	297,	1,797,	1,883,
'58	1,135,	208,	332,	1,907,	2,080,
'59	1,092,	206,	400,	1,903,	2,316,
'60	1,139,	242,	310,	1,905,	2,297,
1861	1,152,	221,	320,	1,927,	2,332,
'62	1,233,	224,	262,	1,914,	2,334,
'63	1,231,	316,	317,	2,070,	2,299,
'64	1,223,	309,	280,	2,110,	2,320,
'65	1,199,	328,	296,	2,102,	2,281,
1866	1,257,	312,	722,	2,521,	2,280,
'67	1,343,	308,	493,	2,372,	2,380,
WALES.					
1856	59,	13,	22,	108,	70,
'57	68,	14,	42,	138,	95,
'58	86,	9,	29,	140,	107,
'59	71,	13,	38,	135,	128,
'60	84,	18,	20,	132,	134,
1861	82,	16,	9,	121,	126,
'62	89,	15,	14,	131,	136,
'63	93,	18,	16,	143,	145,
'64	82,	17,	24,	140,	190,
'65	91,	21,	21,	149,	198,
1866	101,	17,	17,	149,	210,
'67	105,	21,	21,	162,	204,

From the "Miscellaneous Statistics of the United Kingdom," parts ii—vii.

Note. — These returns commence with part ii of the "Miscellaneous "Statistics," dated 1859.

TABLE O.—*Rates of Agricultural Wages in the beneath named Counties of England in the Quarter ending Michaelmas*, 1860.

Districts and Counties.	Rates of Wages for Men, Quarter ended Michaelmas, 1860.			Districts and Counties.	Rates of Wages for Men, Quarter ended Michaelmas, 1860.		
South-Eastern—	*s. d.*	*s.*	*d.*	*West Midland—*	*s. d.*	*s.*	*d.*
Surrey	12 – to	14	–	Gloucestershire	9 – to	10	–
Kent	8 8 „	15	–	Herefordshire	9 –	—	
Sussex	11 – „	12	–	Shropshire	10 –	—	
Southampton	11 – „	15	6	Stafford	13 –	—	
Berkshire	9 – „	15	–	Worcestershire	9 – „	11	–
				Warwickshire	10 6	—	
South Midland—				*North Midland—*			
Herts	10 –	—		Leicestershire	12 – to	15	–
Northamptonshire	11 – to	12	–	Rutland	12 –	—	
Huntingdonshire	10 – „	11	–	Lincoln	13 6	—	
Cambridge	10 –	—		Nottinghamshire	13 6	—	
				Derbyshire	12 –	—	
Eastern—				*North-Western—*			
Essex	10 – to	12	–	Cheshire	11 – to	12	–
Suffolk	9 – „	16	10	Lancashire	13 – „	18	–
Norfolk	10 – „	11	–	*Yorkshire—*			
				West Riding	13 6 to	16	–
				North „	14 – „	15	–
South-Western—				*Northern—*			
Wilts	9 – to	10	–	Durham	13 6 to	15	–
Dorset	9 – „	10	–	Northumberland	15 –	—	
Devonshire	8 – „	12	–	Cumberland	15 –	—	
Cornwall	10 – „	12	–	Westmoreland	12 – „	18	–
Somerset	9 – „	10	6				

Note.—The above are all the English counties and divisions specified in the table whence these rates are extracted. From the "Miscellaneous Statistics of "the United Kingdom," part iii, pp. 271—73.

TABLE P.—*The Highest Amount, and the Last Amount, Levied in Respect of these Four Rates, the Present Valuation of Real Property in respect of which they are Imposed, and the Proportion of the Rates in the £, are respectively as follows.*

Rate.	Highest Amount Returned.		
	Year.	Levied.	Expended.
		£	£
Poor's rate	1818	9,320,000	7,870,801
County ,,	'42	—	1,230,718*
Highway rate {	'11–13 Average 3 years }	1,407,200	1,407,200†
Church ,,	1832	663,814	645,883

Rate.	Latest Amount Returned.			Annual Value of Real Property, 1841.	Rate in the £ by Last Return.	
	Year.	Levied.	Expended.		Levy.	Expenditure.
		£	£	£	s. d.	s. d.
Poor's rate	1842	6,552,890	5,481,053	62,540,030	2 1¼	1 9
County ,,	'42	—	1,230,718*	—	— —	— 5
Highway rate	'39	1,169,891‡	1,169,891	—	— 4½	— 4½
Church ,,	'39	506,812	480,662	—	— 2	— 1¾
Total	—	8,229,593	8,362,324	—	2 7½	2 8

* Amount paid to the county treasurer out of the poor's rate.

† Includes estimated expenditure of statute labour.

‡ There is no return of the amount levied for highway rates, but of course it is not less than the amount expended, which is the sum inserted here.

Note.—Estimate of local taxation in Great Britain and Ireland in the years 1811, 1813, 1818, 1832, 1839, 1842.—"Report of Poor Law Commissioners," 1843.

If to the above amount were added the sums applied by local authorities to local purposes, but raised under a system of taxation different from that which is adverted to in this report, such as the turnpike tolls, the various navigation and port and harbour dues, and the fees paid in the local administration of justice, and in the performance by various local officers of administrative duties, the sums annually disposed of by local authorities in England and Wales would appear much more considerable, and certainly could not be much short of twelve millions of pounds sterling. If again to this were added the amounts raised and disposed of in a similar manner in Scotland and Ireland, the amount would undoubtedly exceed that at the disposal of some of the more important Sovereign States of Europe, for all the purposes both of general and local government.

TABLE Q.—*Local Taxation of England and Wales, Scotland, and Ireland, in 1858-59.*

The following return, "Showing the Amount Annually Collected by " Rates, Tolls, and Dues in England and Wales, Scotland, and Ireland, so " far as the same can be ascertained from existing returns," is obtained from Parl. Paper 204, 1860. The amounts marked * have not been ascertained.

I.—ENGLAND AND WALES.

	£
Poor's rate (with which are collected county police and borough rates), 1858	8,188,880
Church rate (average of seven years)	263,710
(Additional voluntary contributions, 269,550*l*.)	
Highway rate (including paving, &c., under local Acts) 1857	1,949,837
Metropolis Local Management Act—	
Rates levied by general board	159,886
* „ the parishes and district boards....	—
*Local Government Act and Boards of Health (in addition to highways)	—
*Sewers rates, under 3 and 4 Wm. IV, cap. 22	—
*Local Drainage Acts, Bedford Level, Norfolk, Lincoln, &c.	—
*Lighting, &c., Act, 3 and 4 Wm. IV, cap. 90	—
Turnpike tolls, 1856	1,051,050
*Bridge tolls	—
*Ferries	—
*Market tolls and dues	—
*Port dues	—
England and Wales (so far as ascertained), total....	11,613,363

II.—SCOTLAND.

	£	£
By parochial boards (from returns obtained from the Board of Supervision)—		
Under Poor Law Act	622,100	
„ Burial Grounds Act	1,819	
„ Lands Valuation Act	2,704	
„ Registration Act, births, marriages, and deaths	10,240	
„ Nuisances Removal Act	1,462	
		638,325
By counties and burghs (from returns obtained from the Lord Advocate)—		
Rogue money	16,122	
Police force, lighting, and cleansing	214,925	
Prison assessments	32,241	
Roads assessments and paving rates	100,314	
Lands Valuation Act	7,661	
Registration of births, &c.	6,545	
„ voters	3,141	
Nuisances Removal Act	726	
Annuity tax (clergy)	15,017	
Militia stores	12,305	
General municipal expenses	28,291	
		437,288
Turnpike tolls (from Home Office Returns)		209,867
*Statute labour roads		—
Scotland (so far as ascertained), total		1,285,480

TABLE Q.—*Local Taxation of England and Wales, &c.—Contd.*

III.—IRELAND.

	£
From returns obtained from the Lord Lieutenant—	
Grand Jury cess	991,083
Poor rate	526,877
Rates under Towns Improvement Act	10,813
,, Municipal Corporation Act, 3 and 4 Vict., cap. 108	2,409
Lighting and Watching, &c., Act 9 Geo. IV, cap. 82	4,215
Local acts	194,286
Ireland, total	1,729,683

Summary—	£
England and Wales (so far as ascertained)	11,613,363
Scotland	1,285,480
Ireland	1,729,683
United Kingdom, light dues, 1859	273,570
Total (so far as the same has been ascertained)	14,902,096

TABLE R.—*Local Taxation, 1860.*

The items of the following return show the amounts derived from the principal sources of our local taxation, so far as reliable information can be obtained. Although the amounts do not all apply to the same year, I am assured that they are in the main nearly the same as the aggregate amount of any recent year.

In addition to these items, however, there are many others of which it is impossible to estimate the amount with any confidence, such as sewers rates ; lighting and watching rates ; improvement rates ; Metropolitan rates, tolls and dues ; Scotch burgh rates and county assessments.

The returns required under the Local Taxation Returns Act (1860) are, however, fast approaching completion, and these will put an end to all uncertainty.

RATES.

	£
Poor rates, England and Wales, 1859, to Lady-day, 1860	7,715,948
,, Scotland, Whit Sunday, 1859 to 1860	671,516
,, Ireland, Lady-day, 1860	503,813
County receipts, England and Wales, to Michaelmas, 1860	1,222,765
Highways, parish, England and Wales, to 25th March, 1859	2,174,962
Turnpikes, England and Wales, to 31st December, 1858	1,047,308
,, Scotland to Whit Sunday, 1859	238,048
Church rates, 1853-54, England and Wales	482,500
Grand Jury (Ireland) Presentments, 1861	1,034,926
Burgh rates (Scotland), sums paid for prosecutions, 1854	400,000
County police ,,	24,000
Metropolitan (City) rates and duties	200,000
	15,715,786

Note.—Sir S. H. Northcote's " Twenty Years of Financial Policy," p. 399.

TABLE S.—*Showing Amount of Local Taxation Received by each Class of Local Authorities in Ireland in 1869, with the Proportion of each to the whole.*

Classification of Local Authorities in Ireland.	Amount Received.	Proportion of Total Receipts.
	£	Per cnt.
County authorities	1,132,168	39¼
Poor law ,,	830,582	29
Town ,,	487,336	17¼
Harbour ,,	266,196	9½
Inland navigations and drainage authorities	58,528	2¼
Local court authorities	74,574	2½
Four of the special taxes on the trade of pawn-broking	7,619	¼
	2,857,003	100
Deduct under double management	109,226	—
Total	2,747,777	—

TABLE T.—*General Statement of Inland Revenue, Years ending 31st March, 1867-68 and 1868-69.*

Heads of Revenue.	Revenue Raised in Year.	
	1867-68.	1868-69.
	£	£
1. Excise	20,173,288	20,450,386
2. Stamps	9,461,010	9,227,906
3. Taxes	3,450,318	3,484,166
4. Income tax	6,184,166	8,623,507
Total inland revenue	39,268,782	41,785,965

Total revenue from all sources, year ending 31st March, 1869, 72,591,991*l.*
Note.—From " Report of Commissioners of Inland Revenue," 1870.

TABLE U.—*Scotch Poor Law Board Expenditure.*

Period.	Expenditure.					
	Total.	Rate per Head of Population.		Rate per Cent. on Real Property according to Returns in 1843.		
	£	*s.*	*d.*	£	*s.*	*d.*
For year ended 1st February, 1846	295,232	2	3	3	3	4
„ 14th May, 1847	433,915	3	3½	4	13	–
„ „ '48	544,334	4	1¾	5	16	9
„ „ '49	577,044	4	4¾	6	3	9
„ „ '50	581,553	4	5	6	4	9¼
„ „ '51	535,944	3	8	5	14	11¾
„ „ '52	535,868	3	8½	5	14	11¾
„ „ '53	544,553	3	9	5	16	10
„ „ '54	578,929	4	–	6	4	–
„ „ '55	611,785	4	2¾	6	11	3¼
„ „ '56	629,349	4	4¼	6	15	–½
„ „ '57	636,372	4	4¾	6	16	6½
„ „ '58	640,701	4	5	6	17	5¾

Period.	Expenditure.					
	Total.	Rate per Head of Population.		Rate per Cent. on the Annual Value of Real Property according to Returns in 1843.		
	£	*s.*	*d.*	£	*s.*	*d.*
For year ended 14th May, 1859	657,366	4	6½	7	1	–¼
„ „ '60	663,277	4	7	7	2	3¾
„ „ '61	683,902	4	5½	7	6	8¾
„ „ '62	719,317	4	8¼	7	14	4
„ „ '63	736,028	4	9½	7	17	11
„ „ '64	770,030	5	–¼	8	5	2½
„ „ '65	778,274	5	–¾	8	6	11¾
„ „ '66	783,127	5	1¼	8	8	–¼
„ „ '67	807,631	5	3¼	8	13	3½
„ „ '68	863,202	5	7½	9	5	2½
Increase	55,571	–	4¼	–	11	11
Average expenditure for last ten years	746,215	4	10¾	8	–	1

INDEX.

4

HARRISON AND SONS, PRINTERS IN ORDINARY TO HER MAJESTY, ST. MARTIN'S LANE.

www.ingramcontent.com/pod-product-compliance
Lightning Source LLC
Chambersburg PA
CBHW030608270326
41927CB00007B/1089